THE ARAB COLD WAR, 1958–1964

CHATHAM HOUSE ESSAYS

Previous essays in the series have been:

The Royal Institute of International Affairs is an unofficial body which promotes the scientific study of international questions and does not express opinions of its own. The opinions expressed in this publication are the responsibility of the author.

The Institute gratefully acknowledges the comments and suggestions of the following who read the manuscript on behalf of the Research Committee: Elie Kedourie, Professor Bernard Lewis, and A. H. Hourani.

The Arab Cold War
1958-1964

A STUDY OF IDEOLOGY IN POLITICS

BY

MALCOLM KERR

*Issued under the auspices of the
Royal Institute of International Affairs*
OXFORD UNIVERSITY PRESS
LONDON   NEW YORK   TORONTO
1965

Oxford University Press, Amen House, London E.C.4

GLASGOW   NEW YORK   TORONTO   MELBOURNE   WELLINGTON
BOMBAY   CALCUTTA   MADRAS   KARACHI   LAHORE   DACCA
CAPE TOWN   SALISBURY   NAIROBI   IBADAN   ACCRA
KUALA LUMPUR   HONG KONG

DS
38
K38

Printed in Great Britain by
The Bowering Press, Plymouth

Contents

Sources

THIS book is not intended to be a history but an interpretative essay. It is based on a limited number of published documents, Arab press and radio materials, and standard reference periodicals, and does not purport to represent exhaustive research.

Chapter 3, dealing with the Cairo negotiations of March and April 1963, draws almost exclusively on the transcript of the talks published by the Egyptian authorities under the title *Mahadir jalsat mubahathat al-wahda* (Cairo, National Printing and Publishing House, 1963, 602 pp). Except where indicated, the passages of direct quotation are reproduced from the abridged translation published in *Arab Political Documents, 1963* (American University of Beirut, Department of Political Studies and Public Administration, 1964), with the kind permission of the editors. Other materials from this very useful source are cited extensively in Chapter 4. The spelling of Arabic names has been adapted to conform to the system used elsewhere in this essay, for the reader's convenience.

Radio broadcast quotations are taken, with occasional adaptation, from unpublished translations to which I had access in the United States; interested British readers can also consult the BBC *Summary of World Broadcasts*, Part IV. Reference periodicals consulted include *Les Cahiers de l'Orient contemporain* (Paris), *Orient* (Paris), *Chronology of Arab Politics* (American University of Beirut), and *President Gamal Abdel-Nasser's Speeches and Press-Interviews* (annual, Cairo). For other materials I have relied in occasional instances on the Arab newspaper press, as cited: *L'Orient* (Beirut), *al-Ba'th* (Damascus), and *al-Ahram* (Cairo).

Additional information was kindly supplied in inter-views by Lt-General Luay al-Atasi and Messrs Salah al-Din al-Bitar, Akram Dayri, Nazih al-Hakim, Hani al-Hindi, Muhsin Ibrahim, Nihad al-Qasim, and Talib Husayn Shabib. None of them is responsible for any of the judgements expressed in this book.

I

Trial and Error: The United Arab Republic, 1958-61

*Will anyone accept Aleppo as separate from Damascus?
Is there any real difference between this separation and the
separation of Damascus from Cairo?*
AHMAD BAHA AL-DIN, *Akhbar al-Yawm*, 16 May 1962

EVER since the second world war popular political sentiment in the Arab world has been dominated by urgent
appeals for Arab unity, while the field of activity between
governments and parties has been dominated by bitter
rivalry. Why the idea of unity is so strong among Arabs—
so much more than among Latin Americans, for instance,
or the English-speaking nations—is a mystery that neither
Arab nor western historians have satisfactorily explained.
In this essay we shall content ourselves with acknowledg-
ing that this obsession, whatever its causes, is an important
psychological force, and therefore a political reality, which
warring politicians seek to use against each other. Our
purpose is to study one phase of this curious phenomenon,
namely Egyptian-Syrian relations from the creation of the
United Arab Republic in February 1958 to the Arab
Summit Conference of January 1964. More particularly,
we are concerned with President Gamal 'Abd al-Nasir's
relations with the Ba'th Party of Syria, which reached
their decisive stage in 1963.

The idea of pan-Arabism since the war has been closely
bound up with two other leading ideas. One of these is
anti-colonialism; the other is revolutionary socialism.

While these two ideas have overlapped considerably with each other, it is useful to make a rough chronological division between them.

Anti-colonialism

Hostility to Western influence was the principal ideological companion of pan-Arabism until about 1958, that is to say until the main channels of British and American power in inter-Arab affairs were destroyed with the Syrian-Egyptian union and in the aftermath of the Iraqi revolution and the Lebanese civil war. From 1945 to 1958, first Britain and France, then Britain and the United States, had been deeply involved in relations among Egypt, Syria, Iraq, Jordan, Lebanon, and Saudi Arabia. The Western powers acted not always successfully, and sometimes at cross-purposes, but usually in such a manner that the Arabs were acutely conscious of their involvement. From 1955 to 1958 the Soviet Union was also active, lending her weight to the Syrian and Egyptian governments and then to the Iraqi revolution, as a counter to the support given to other regimes by Britain and America.

An account of the inter-Arab struggle in the years preceding the formation of the UAR would be out of place here. It is sufficient to emphasize that the centre of the contest for influence in the Arab world was in Syria, and that the principal protagonists were Iraq and Egypt. This competition began well before the Egyptian revolution of 1952, and at heart it had nothing to do with ideology. It was a geopolitical struggle, reminiscent of countless occasions in the distant past when rulers of the Nile and Mesopotamian valleys had disputed control of the area lying between them. In more immediate terms the competition went back to the end of the second world war. With the termination of French colonial authority, Syria had become free to choose her alignments within the Arab world, and other Arab states were free to try to influence her. Partly for reasons of sentiment and dynastic ambition dating from the first world war and partly because of the urge to promote Iraqi leadership among the Arabs, the principal Iraqi leaders—the Regent, Prince 'Abd al-Ilah, and the perennial Prime Minister, Nuri al-Sa'id—sought on repeated occasions to bring about a Syrian-Iraqi unification under the Hashimite crown or, failing that, a close alliance. Correspondingly they were opposed on each occasion by the Egyptian government of the day and by Saudi Arabia.

Differing relationships with Britain accentuated this rivalry. The Iraqi regime was enthusiastically allied with Britain, while a series of Egyptian governments sought to bring their British treaty to an end. A constant object of British Middle East policy was to maintain a strong and friendly Iraq, and the interests of Iraq and Britain in the future of Syria were closely associated. As Egypt resisted the efforts of Iraq, so France, until 1956, resisted those of Britain: for the French were jealous of the commercial, cultural, and political influence that had remained to them after the collapse of their Syrian mandate, and they did not forget the role Britain had played during the war in bringing the collapse about. Among Syrian politicians and soldiers were those with ties of various kinds with the French, the British, the Egyptians, the Saudis, or the Iraqis. Some took subsidies from several directions, and others harboured a distrust of all outside parties. And from 1955 onwards the game was joined by the United States and the Soviet Union as well.

Throughout these years pro-Iraqi Syrian politicians operated under serious handicaps. Republican sentiment in Syria was strong, and in the minds of many—particularly the younger educated generation who began to swell the ranks of the politically conscious after the war—British influence was as odious as French. They remembered that 'Abd ul-Ilah, Nuri al-Sa'id, and their associates had been rescued from overthrow in 1941 only by British military intervention, and they also blamed Britain for the Arab disaster in Palestine, about which they cared deeply. Any union with Iraq, they argued, would link Syria with the imperialists and would actually forestall further steps towards Arab unity, since both Britain and the Hashimite royal house would insist on restricting unity to those Arab countries they could hope to control: Iraq, Syria, and Jordan. Egypt, the largest and strongest Arab state, would be permanently excluded. While Egypt held no particular appeal to Syrian opinion—it was not until 1955 that Gamal 'Abd al-Nasir emerged as a pan-Arab hero—she had at least gained sympathy for her efforts to throw off British domination; and what the Egyptians constantly sought in Damascus was not outright union, but only that Syria should keep Iraq at arm's length. This limited objective was within their reach.

A series of domestic and international crises from 1949 through 1957 provided the occasions for efforts in and out of Syria to push the country in one direction or the other. A staple ingredient in this process was the chronic involvement of the Syrian army in politics, beginning with the three consecutive coups d'état of 1949. Further coups occurred in 1952 and 1954; at other times military cliques intervened in the affairs of state in less overt ways, or carried on struggles against each other in order to determine which one would have its way with the civilians. Competing politicians meanwhile deliberately cultivated friends in the army and on occasion encouraged military intervention in support of their own factional interests. Civilians and officers alike also appealed to patrons in various Arab and foreign capitals, thus internationalizing

even those conflicts that were of a purely domestic origin
and reinforcing the inclination of outsiders to involve
themselves in Syrian affairs.[1]

The 1950s witnessed a series of major attempts by
Britain and the United States to bolster their strategic
interests in the region. The means that they chose closely
involved Syria and exacerbated her domestic tensions.
Each of these efforts failed, and in the process served to
accentuate anti-Western sentiment in Syria and other
Arab countries. In 1951 came the proposal for a combined
British, French, American, Turkish, and Egyptian Middle
East Defence Organization, into which Syria, Iraq, and
others would presumably be drawn. The plan came to
nothing when the Egyptian government adamantly rejected it.

In 1955 Britain, Iraq, Turkey, Iran, and Pakistan
created the Baghdad Pact for the purpose of regional
defence. The chief British interest in the Pact was to provide a substitute for the expiring Anglo-Iraqi treaty, which
was judged to be feasible only within a multilateral framework. The Iraqi authorities were eager to renew their
British ties, but they faced the prospect of isolation within
the Arab League and mounting condemnation by Arab
opinion unless other Arab partners could be brought in—
in particular, Syria and Jordan—and Egyptian hostility
warded off. The Syrian coup of 1954, which had removed
the Egyptian-leaning dictatorship of Brigadier Adib
Shishakli and put in its place a civilian parliamentary
regime of diverse and fluctuating orientations, made the
hope of drawing Syria into the Pact seem plausible.

But given the strength of neutralist and anti-Hashimite
sentiment in Syria, it seems doubtful that this effort ever
had a chance of more than temporary success. As it turned

[1] For a first-class detailed account of this subject see Patrick Seale, *The
Struggle for Syria* (1965).

out, it met with no success at all. The Baghdad Pact was loudly denounced in Cairo from the beginning, with reverberations in Jordan, Lebanon, and Syria. A combination of Egyptian, Saudi, and Soviet blandishments swung Syria away from the Pact, and before 1955 was out she had signed a military alliance with Egypt and purchased arms from the Soviets.

The position of Syrian politicians friendly to Iraq, Britain, and the United States was virtually destroyed by the Suez affair and other Western blunders that accompanied or followed it, such as the Eisenhower Doctrine of 1957 by which the United States declared that the need of the hour was to defend the Middle East against the aggression of 'states controlled by international Communism'. The Lebanese, Jordanian, and Saudi governments allowed themselves to become open allies of the United States and condemned Cairo and Damascus for allegedly opening the door to the spread of Communism in the area. They were rewarded with American arms and money, but both they and their patrons paid the price of widespread protest and condemnation. This helped pave the way for the armed insurrection that plunged Lebanon into anarchy beginning in May 1958 and the military coup that liquidated the Iraqi monarchy two months later. Meanwhile Syria was martyred by her encirclement. When in September 1957 American officials suggested that Syria was slipping towards Communism and encouraged the Turks to mass their army on the Syrian frontier, the Russians and Egyptians gained the opportunity to pin the label of 'aggression' once again on the Western powers and their local 'stooges'. It was Egypt and the Soviet Union alone to whom the Syrians could turn to rescue them from their isolation.

The issue of Syria's orientation was settled, apparently for good, by her union with Egypt in February 1958. With this step the pressures of Britain, the United States, Iraq, and (from the other side) the Soviet Union on domestic Syrian affairs ended. The Iraqi revolution of July 1958 eliminated Britain's position there, and the subsequent landing of American and British troops in Lebanon and Jordan respectively, to forestall a chain reaction that might overthrow the regimes in those countries, was the last major Western effort to play a decisive role in inter-Arab affairs. From 1959 onwards, apart from one or two peripheral exceptions, the crucial decisions governing Arab affairs lay in Arab hands.

Revolutionary socialism

Increasingly after 1958 the attraction of Arab unity came to be accompanied by the idea of revolutionary socialism, which has tended to overshadow the anti-colonial spirit in ideological discourses and pronouncements. There is no sharp dividing line here: anti-colonialism has remained a rallying-cry since 1958, and long before that date radical currents had been gathering force in domestic Arab politics. But there was a shift in emphasis which was accentuated by the advent of the United Arab Republic and the Iraqi revolution. Increasingly the enemies of Arabism were held to be the 'reactionaries'—hereditary monarchs, oligarchic politicians, and wealthy landowners and businessmen—who found it easier to obstruct reforms by keeping the Arab world divided. Their alleged co-operation with the imperialists was held to be simply a facet of their reactionary outlook.

In the new Syrian-Egyptian union the ideas of revolutionary socialism acquired particular significance from the character of the union's principal architects, Gamal 'Abd al-Nasir and the Arab Socialist Resurrection (Ba'th) Party of Syria. Their ideological outlooks appeared indistinguishable: both believed in the imperative need for the removal of all vestiges of foreign control in the Arab world and in an Arab foreign policy of non-alignment between the Great Powers, in comprehensive Arab unity, and in social, political, and economic reconstruction under the stimulus of state action. Both believed that these objectives were closely related in practice to each other, and could only be achieved by revolutionary means. In these respects a marriage between 'Abd al-Nasir and the Ba'th seemed eminently suitable. But each came into the union with a distinct background of experience and distinct expectattions.

'Abd al-Nasir had risen to power at the head of a military coup. He and his principal colleagues were all soldiers, graduates of the Egyptian military academy in the late 1930s, and they approached Egypt's problems with the proverbial distaste of military men for intellectual theorizing. They sensed, increasingly as time passed, that the list of ills to be remedied in Egypt was endless, but they approached specific ills in a pragmatic spirit with whatever means came to hand. Their initial ideology, to the extent they had one at all, was primitive and general: they were against corruption, social oppression, and imperialism, and they proposed to clean up the country, strengthen the army, build up the economy, broaden opportunities for the lower classes, and—when they were ready—institute a 'clean' democracy. They distrusted political parties, not for any reason of dogma but because the parties they had known in pre-revolutionary Egypt had been the vehicles of a corrupt oligarchy. Accordingly they dissolved all existing parties, and as a substitute means for gathering public support for themselves, they created a mass organization called the Liberation Rally. But they did not take this very seriously and until 1956 they ran the country openly as a military dictatorship, through their Revolutionary Command Council comprising the dozen or so most important officers. When the union with Syria was formed the Egyptian leaders had only very recently begun to experiment with constitutional life: a parliament had been chosen in a carefully screened election, and the first steps had barely been taken towards creating what they hoped would be a more dynamic mass movement than the Liberation Rally, to be named the National Union.

Socialism in Egypt evolved in the 1950s as a series of improvised programmes rather than as an ideology. The military leaders had decreed agrarian, labour, educational, and other reforms in response to specific needs and generally in order to win public support for themselves. The first incursions of the state into management of the industrial and commercial economy came as byproducts of the international crisis of 1956: the regime found itself in control of the Suez Canal administration and a large number of enterprises sequestered from their British and French owners. Subsequently, in the wake of this experience, the revolutionary government developed a growing taste for state planning and ownership, which eventually culminated in the socialist decrees of July 1961, shortly before the end of the union with Syria; and from then on 'Abd al-Nasir became considerably more doctrinaire in his ideology. But at the time the union was formed, explicitly socialist ideas and programmes were only vaguely beginning to take shape. What 'Abd al-Nasir brought to the union, then, was not a radical ideology but a talent for leadership, the experience of five and a half eventful and difficult, but successful, years in authority, and unrivalled personal prestige.

The Syrian Ba'th and Communists

The Ba'th Party that propelled Syria into union with Egypt was the product of a merger, in December 1952, between what had originally been two distinct parties. One of these, the original Ba'th Party, had been founded a decade earlier by two Paris-educated school teachers, Salah al-Din al-Bitar and Michel 'Aflaq. It was especially the latter who gave the party its intellectual character and appeal, in his press editorials, lectures, and books. 'One Arab Nation with an Eternal Mission' proclaimed the party's principal slogan. 'Aflaq and Bitar had flirted with Communism in Paris, then had renounced it upon becoming convinced of its incompatibility with nationalism. None the less, Marxism had left a permanent imprint on their ideas: not only dialectics and socialism, but a penchant for chiliastic visions and doctrines and for an evangelistic approach to politics. The Arab Nation required liberation, unity, and socialism, and these were not only interdependent goals but aspects of a single undefinable metaphysical reality. In fact, the Arab Nation required not only these things but something transcending them: a spiritual rebirth, a transformation. Hence the name 'Ba'th': the party of the Resurrection, or Renaissance. Perhaps 'Aflaq's Christian origin played an unacknowledged part in these ideas.

The other tributary of the united party was Akram al-Hawrani's Arab Socialist Party, based on his electoral stronghold in the north Syrian city of Hama. Whereas 'Aflaq was a reflective, sensitive, painfully shy intellectual, affectionately known to his younger followers as 'the Professor', Hawrani was an eminently practical political tactician and man of action who had survived a long series of successive connexions with diverse political groups and leaders. A man of little education and no interest in systematic doctrines, he none the less shared with 'Aflaq and Bitar an instinct for revolutionary causes. His local reputation in Hama had been made as a bitter enemy of the great landed families of the region. It was Hawrani who supplied the Ba'th Party after 1952 with most of its following in the army, for he had cultivated friendships and exchanged radical ideas with a number of younger officers for many years. After collaborating with Brigadier Adib Shishakli's dictatorship for a time, he broke with him in 1952 and took refuge in Lebanon, in company with 'Aflaq and Bitar. Some of the officers who overthrew Shishakli in 1954 were Hawrani's special friends, particularly Colonel Mustafa Hamdun. These and other officers, in co-operation with the civilian leadership of the Ba'th, played a crucial role in January 1958 in travelling to Cairo and persuading 'Abd al-Nasir in the name of the Syrian army that only immediate unity with Egypt could save Syria from anarchy.

Thus the Ba'th had something of a dual personality as a legacy of its origins. After the break-up of the UAR in 1961 it was to split in two once again. But in any case its character differed greatly from that of 'Abd al-Nasir's regime. Thanks to 'Aflaq and Bitar, and despite Hawrani's unconcern, it was an avowedly doctrinaire party with a specifically revolutionary, socialist, pan-Arabist creed. Its membership was limited but militant, well organized, and largely university educated. Furthermore, the party was not confined to Syria, though its headquarters were there: it had branches in Lebanon, Jordan, and Iraq. The practical political experience of the Ba'th leaders had been primarily confined to electioneering and to activity in parliament, where Hawrani had sat off and on since 1943 and where in the 1954 elections the party gained control of 22 of 142 seats. Hawrani and 'Aflaq had each briefly held office as cabinet ministers in 1949–50; Bitar was

Syrian Foreign Minister from June 1956 until the union
with Egypt, and in 1957 Hawrani became Speaker of Parliament. As a minority parliamentary party in the 1950s,
the Ba'th were accustomed to dealing with the more conservative groups of politicians who dominated the parliament in the shifting alignments and coalitions that had
long been characteristic of Syrian constitutional life, and
although much of their influence within parliament was
due to their connexions in the army, especially in the last
two years, the 'Aflaq–Bitar wing of the Ba'th harboured a
considerable mistrust of military interventions in politics.

Ironically, it was not the practical-minded Egyptian
junta but the Ba'th, with its doctrinaire teachings of revolutionary socialism, who had spent the last years before
1958 in collaboration with 'reactionaries'. From 1955
Syrian foreign policy was closely aligned both with Egypt
and the Soviet Union. But at the same time many of the
principal politicians in office, including President Shukri
al-Quwatli, the Prime Minister, Sabri al-'Asali, and the
Deputy Prime Minister, Khalid al-'Azm, were oligarchs
of the old school. The Syrian Communist Party was
represented in parliament only by its leader, Khalid Bak-
dash. The Syrian economic system continued to be one of
laisser-faire, under which the country had enjoyed a remarkable span of prosperity since the war; and it seemed
somewhat anomalous that such a man as Khalid al-'Azm,
a scion of one of Damascus's oldest and most distinguished
families and the owner of vast landed properties which he
showed no inclination to renounce, should acquire the
nickname of 'the Red Pasha' by championing friendship
with the Soviet Union and by his prominence as a negotiator of Soviet military and economic aid.

Yet despite this façade of domestic conservatism, real
power in Syria drifted increasingly into the hands of the
Ba'th, the Communists, and their respective sympathizers,

especially in the army. In the summer of 1957 an officer with Communist affiliations, Colonel 'Afif al-Bizri, became Army Chief of Staff. Other officers in important positions were either Ba'th members or sympathizers or, like the Chief of Military Intelligence, Colonel 'Abd al-Hamid Sarraj, held comparable radical nationalist views and were considered friends of the party. The traditional politicians in office were increasingly carried along by the pressures applied to them by cliques of ideologues and soldiers. The variety of political factions on the Syrian scene in 1954 was progressively reduced over the next four years as one after another—the conspiratorial Syrian National Social Party, the Muslim Brotherhood, the conservative People's Party—were discredited for various reasons. The National Party politicians, including President Quwatli and the Prime Minister, al-'Asali, as well as various independents such as Khalid al-'Azm, remained on the scene. Some of them, Quwatli especially, still benefited from the prestige they had acquired in opposing the French before independence and the Baghdad Pact, and in co-operating with Egypt. But individually they had become inappropriate symbols of a revolutionary age: too old, too bourgeois, too comfortable, too much machine politicians, too easily caricatured by the cartoonist (paunchy, perspiring, wearing thick-lensed glasses, a fez, and a broad-striped double-breasted suit like those worn by provincial French businessmen, and fingering a set of amber prayer-beads).

There remained the Communists and the Ba'th, rival aspirants to revolutionary leadership. With the field largely cleared of other contestants, the tactical collaboration that they had practised for a time now came to an end. It seems doubtful that control of either the government or the army was even remotely within reach of the Syrian Communists, had they been bold enough to try;

and the explanation widely circulated afterwards that the Ba'th had sought union with 'Abd al-Nasir in order to avert a Communist take-over probably concealed a more complex reality. It is possible that the Ba'th and their friends feared that the combined pressures and intrigues coming from Syria's pro-Western neighbours would sooner or later be exploited by the Syrian Communists, the Soviet government, and Khalid al-'Azm and his fellow 'progressives' in order to claim a more substantial share of power, and that it might prove possible to resist such claims only with the aid of the Western powers and their hated Middle Eastern friends—aid for which a price must be paid. In any case, appealing to Cairo for union seemed to pan-Arab Syrians to be an act not of surrender but of triumph. What had they been advocating for so many years, if not unity with a strong, progressive, revolutionary fellow Arab state?[2]

The Syrian-Egyptian union

The circumstances and rationale of the Syrian-Egyptian union involved certain ambiguous considerations. As 'Abd al-Nasir reminded the Syrian leaders at the 1963 unity talks, in 1958 he had initially resisted the whole idea of union. He had argued that Syria must first find her own internal unity, that the ground between the two countries must be prepared, and that another five years' time was needed. At length he did consent to an immediate union, but on certain conditions. It should not be a federal union as some Syrians preferred, but a heavily centralized one. The army must renounce further involvement in politics; all political parties must be dissolved. His terms were accepted. President Quwatli and Prime

[2] Extended discussions of the circumstances in which unity was negotiated may be found in the final chapter of Seale, *Struggle for Syria*, and in ch. 11 of Gordon Torrey, *Syrian Politics and the Military, 1945–1958* (1964).

Minister 'Asali passively assented to negotiations that the Ba'th and friends in the army had initiated; Khalid al-'Azm and the Communists both manoeuvred against the union, frantically but ineffectively. After the union was consumated on 22 February 1958, Shukri al-Quwatli retired with the honorific status of 'First Citizen of the UAR', 'Asali became an ornamental Vice-President in Cairo, 'Azm retired from politics, and the Communists went underground.

The centralization of authority in 'Abd al-Nasir's hands made good sense inasmuch as it had been the Syrians' despair of governing themselves any longer that had precipitated the union. On the other hand, events were to show that Nasir had been right in the first instance in objecting that the road was dangerously unprepared. All would presumably be well if he could find effective and congenial Syrian allies. In the circumstances these would have to be sought primarily in the Ba'th Party, who as kindred revolutionary spirits might be presumed to be natural partners but with whom, in practice, 'Abd al-Nasir's relations were altogether untested.

In this context we must consider the ambiguity of the Ba'th's expectations at the time of the union. On what basis and in what degree could they expect to share effective power with their Egyptian partners? While on the one hand they sought union in a spirit of desperation and fear of their own inability to maintain control in Syria, on the other hand they seem to have imagined that once the union was formed, they would not only see their rivals eliminated through the weight of 'Abd al-Nasir's prestige, but that they would also hold their own against him. It was all too reminiscent of the joke a decade ago about Frenchmen who wanted Germany to have an army larger than that of Russia but smaller than that of France.

This brings us to the heart of the difficulties and misunderstandings between President 'Abd al-Nasir and the Ba'th both during the period of Syro-Egyptian union and later on, in 1963, when an unsuccessful effort was made to negotiate a second union. The Ba'th was an ideological party, and its leaders suffered the common illusion of ideologues everywhere that they possessed a unique vision of the Truth, which was somehow indispensable for effective political action and which could somehow be converted into political power. Nasir had admirable revolutionary instincts, but, as Michel 'Aflaq indiscreetly told the press just after the inauguration of the union, he was in need of a 'philosophy'. This, implicitly, the Ba'th would provide. They could see that their slogans of 'liberation, unity, socialism' were being adopted in practice by the Egyptian regime and that a general identity of revolutionary orientation existed, but 'Abd al-Nasir's policies, because they were improvised and pragmatic rather than doctrinaire, were thought by Ba'thists to be, at heart, undisciplined, opportunistic, and open to contradictions. For what revolution could be preserved without a guiding creed? Surely before long Nasir would be brought by his own experience to acknowledge this need, and would turn to the Ba'th. (We shall see that in 1963 Nasir was to fling this proposition back in the faces of 'Aflaq and Bitar.)

On this basis the Ba'thists expected to perform valuable services for the Egyptian leader and to enjoy a commensurate influence, not only in Syria but throughout the future Arab union, which hopefully before very long would extend beyond Egypt and Syria. For the time being, at any rate, at least they could hope to be entrusted with the management of the Syrian province on behalf of the new union. After all, no other eligible group was in sight; and ideology aside, the Ba'th possessed an organization with experienced personnel and an ability to keep in touch with popular opinion. It did not disturb the Ba'th leaders that 'Abd al-Nasir would require the dissolution of all Syrian political parties, including their own, to make room for the creation both in Egypt and Syria of a single state-sponsored party, the National Union. They readily assented to this in the belief that it would be largely left to them to organize this new body in their own fashion. 'We will be officially dissolved', said 'Aflaq in the statement to the press already referred to. 'But we will be present in the new unified party, the National Union. As the child of the union of the two countries, this movement cannot be animated by principles other than those of the Ba'th.'[3]

Retrospectively it seems that President 'Abd al-Nasir might have done better to accept this arrangement. The National Union, no matter how rapidly established, could not acquire a life of its own by presidential fiat but must depend for its vitality on the already existing talents, reputations, and connexions of its leading members. At the time of the union the Ba'th and the Communists were the only organized forces that counted for much in Syrian politics. There were, of course, many other prominent and active individuals, military and civilian, but these exerted what influence they had increasingly within the orbit of the two parties. Even Colonel 'Abd al-Hamid Sarraj, perhaps the most powerful individual in Syria on the eve of the union, had built up his position not only through his command of military intelligence and his influence on other individual officers, but also through cultivating a close association from 1955 onwards with the Ba'th leaders, particularly Akram Hawrani. 'Abd al-Nasir himself hinted, years later, that he regretted not relying on the Ba'th more heavily: in the course of the 1963 unity talks, he said that the wholesale dissolution of parties had been a

[3] Quoted in Simon Jargy, 'Le Déclin d'un parti', *Orient* (Paris), xi/3 (1959), p. 29.

tactical mistake that had left a vacuum at the heart of the National Union, and that it would have been better to have formed a national front among existing nationalist progressive forces. In practice, such a front could only have been dominated by the Ba'th.

In the event, however, 'Abd al-Nasir did not adopt this view. Parties in Egypt had long since been abolished, and it must have seemed only consistent to do the same in Syria. As for the Ba'thists' ideological self-consciousness, he may have found this slightly pretentious and certainly did not feel himself in need of moral guidance from intellectuals. He did appoint individual Ba'thists to high office. Hawrani was made a Vice-President of the Republic and Chairman of the Executive Council for the Syrian province, with Ba'thist Ministers of Economy and Social Affairs under him. Salah al-Din Bitar was brought to Cairo and made a Minister of State and later Minister of Culture and National Guidance in the central cabinet. But on the question of controlling the creation of the National Union organization, the Ba'th failed to obtain a free hand. Certainly this was not for lack of trying, and later the complaint was made that throughout 1958 Ba'thist leaders had repeatedly obstructed attempts to set in motion the creation of the organization, out of dissatisfaction with the proposed terms. In this connexion it was noteworthy that Colonel Sarraj, as regional Minister of the Interior and thus closely involved in the process, was much less cooperative with the Ba'thists after the union than before, and in fact his standing in Cairo rose as theirs declined.

The price for this failure was paid entirely by the Ba'th. At issue was the manner in which elections would be conducted for the local committees of the National Union. It would have been possible to provide for the screening of prospective candidates and the elimination of a considerable number before the election, as had been done in the

Egyptian parliamentary elections of 1957. Such a process could, of course, have been manipulated to the Ba'thists' advantage. Even without these formal means, conservative antagonists of the Ba'th of the traditional school could have been quietly discouraged here and there. None of these steps were taken, however, and when elections were finally scheduled for 8 July 1959—some seventeen months after the UAR came into existence—Ba'th leaders panicked, first calling on their candidates to withdraw, then changing their minds and after all running in a reduced number of localities. On election day they did poorly. The principal leaders were all successful, but throughout Syria only an estimated 250 Ba'thists were elected out of a total of 9,445 seats.

Particularly galling was the fact that in many places they were opposed and defeated by coalitions of conservatives, who capitalized on holding the Ba'th responsible for the many incidental inconveniences and irritations that the union with Egypt had unavoidably inflicted on the Syrian populace; for it was the Ba'th, after all, that had taken the lead in precipitating the union in the first place. It seemed, ironically, as if 'Abd al-Nasir, the revolutionary dictator whose cause the Ba'th had supported so ardently, had chosen to undermine them with the help of 'reactionaries' by the most democratic of means, a free election. This was the ultimate indignity. Presumably some Ba'thists felt a certain bitter satisfaction, after the collapse of the union in 1961, in hearing Nasir blame the disaster partly on the 'infiltration of reactionaries' into the committees of the National Union.

The position of the Ba'th, undercut in the elections, deteriorated rapidly. First, in August 1959, there was a split in the party. A party congress meeting in mysterious circumstances in Lebanon expelled the two leading Jordanian members, 'Abdullah Rimawi and Bahjat Abu

Ghuraiba.[4] These men subsequently went to Cairo and organized a splinter 'Ba'th' Party of their own.

The next month President 'Abd al-Nasir relieved Riyad al-Malki of his post of Minister of National Guidance. Despairing of maintaining further influence in the government, the remaining Ba'thists in leading positions—Hawrani, Bitar, Mustafa Hamdun, and 'Abd al-Ghani Qannut—resigned *en bloc* at the end of December, thus bringing to an end the chapter of Ba'th collaboration with the Egyptian leadership. Years later Secretary-General 'Aflaq was to tell 'Abd al-Nasir that this action had been taken on the basis of a party decision in which he had participated, despite the fact that the party was officially dissolved, and to admit that he had unsuccessfully tried to induce several Egyptian ministers to leave the government at the same time. Nasir took the collective resignation as an almost treasonable affront.[5] The Ba'th summed up their complaints in veiled ideological language:

What the union needed was to encourage the popular wave in Syria, and to benefit from the experience and [intellectual] wealth of that country in order to facilitate its integration with Egypt, where a great revolutionary and popular vacuum existed. The fact is that the Egyptian popular movement, smothered before the revolution by the duplicity of the politicians, was unable to revive itself in a sound manner afterwards.[6]

The elections and resignations dramatized the contrasting interpretations of 'Abd al-Nasir and the Ba'th leaders of the terms of the unity agreement and the manner in which the newly established institutions were to operate. In part it was a case of clashing ambitions, in the sense

[4] For further details of the congress see ibid., pp. 33 ff.

[5] See below, Ch. 3.

[6] Editorial in the Beirut Ba'thist newspaper *al-Sahafa*, 22 Feb. 1960. The above quotation is from the French trans. in *Orient*, xiii/1 (1960), pp. 142–6.

that in practice each side was claiming the right to run Syria as it saw fit. In part it was a divergence of calculations. The Ba'th had expected Nasir to sense a need for their services, whereas in fact, rightly or wrongly, he did not. It was on substantially the same grounds that the two sides were destined to fall out with each other once more in 1963. The events of 1958–9 in any case demonstrated how inconsequential ideological ties can be in Arab politics in the face of the will to power of rival individuals and factions, and the shifts and divergences of their tactical requirements.

Egypt and the Arab world

The Ba'thists had been dismayed not only by President 'Abd al-Nasir's methods of government within the union, but also by his policies in the outer Arab world. Here was a further instance in which relations between Nasir and the Ba'th were coloured by a mixture of ideological and practical considerations. In February 1958 both Egypt's and Syria's relations with their conservatively ruled and pro-Western neighbours—Iraq, Jordan, Saudi Arabia, Lebanon, and Turkey, to say nothing of Israel—had been deplorable, and it was partly in order to rescue the Syrian regime from its insecurity that the UAR had been formed. The wave of exuberance that swept Syria at the start of the union, signified by the triumphant crowds that welcomed Nasir to Damascus, and widely shared by Arab opinion in the surrounding Arab states, reflected a conviction that the tables had been turned, that the initiative in the Middle East had passed to the revolutionary pan-Arab movement, that before long the peoples of other Arab states would rise up against their tyrannical rulers and join the union. There was a compelling sense of destiny in this attitude, not least among Syrians, including the Ba'thists who had helped negotiate the unity agreement. It was not simply a Syro-Egyptian union, but the first stone that would start the avalanche of a more comprehensive Arab unity. When the Hashimite rulers of Jordan and Iraq countered a few days later by hastily signing a federal union between themselves, the pan-Arabists confidently dismissed this as a stop-gap arrangement between reactionaries who lacked the support of their subjects. The uprising in Lebanon against President Sham'un's government that began in May, and then the Iraqi revolution of 14 July that put an end to the monarchy, brought pan-Arab expectations to their height, and momentarily it seemed as if the predestined day were at hand.

Then the expectations turned sour. American troops landed in Lebanon and British troops in Jordan. Sham'un left office, but peacefully at the end of his term, and was succeeded by a compromise regime that would secure the continuation of Lebanese independence. King Husayn in Jordan survived to fight another day. The gravest disappointment was in Iraq. 'Abd al-Nasir's picture suddenly blossomed forth in Baghdad shop windows on 14 July; then almost as quickly it disappeared. It had not been a straightforward Arab nationalist revolution but an explosion of the discontent of many political and social elements of Iraq's fragmented society against the old oligarchy: Kurds and Shi'ites as well as Sunni Arabs, Communists as well as nationalists. The coalition of which the new regime was composed soon descended to an internal struggle in which the Arab nationalists, including the Iraqi branch of the Ba'th Party, lost out and found that their influence in the country was replaced by that of Communists and fellow-travellers. The leading Arab nationalist figure, Colonel 'Abd al-Salam 'Arif, two days after the revolution stood on a balcony in Damascus with

Gamal 'Abd al-Nasir to receive the cheers of the crowd; three months later he was in a Baghdad jail under sentence of death. By the end of the year relations between Iraq and the UAR were even worse than they had been in the days of the old regime. In the Iraqi 'People's Court', the revolutionary tribunal established to try members of the former government, the fellow-travelling president, Colonel Mahdawi, turned the proceedings into a circus with his sarcastic asides against President 'Abd al-Nasir; and Nasir, for his part, delivered bitter speeches denouncing the Iraqi prime minister, Major-General 'Abd al-Karim Qasim, as a traitor to Arab nationalism and a stooge of international Communism. The low point in Baghdad–Cairo relations was reached in March 1959 when an uprising in the Iraqi city of Mosul, led by Arab nationalist officers and supported by the UAR, was bloodily suppressed. The next autumn there was an unsuccessful attempt on Qasim's life, attributed to agents of the UAR. From that time onwards, until February 1963, when the situation settled down to a dreary and inconclusive cold war between Cairo and Baghdad, sporadically punctuated by the trading of insults. Inside Iraq, Qasim presided over a strange regime that drifted in a twilight zone between Communism and a shapeless, anarchic radicalism, resting on no visible organized support and held together largely by the bafflement of all potential challengers of the 'Faithful Leader' in seeking an appropriate ground on which to confront him.

The problem for the UAR government was that Qasim was an Arab revolutionary whose behaviour defied conventional expectations and explanations. He failed to cooperate in the march towards Arab unity, or even to pay President 'Abd al-Nasir any of the respect that other revolutionary leaders did; he threw Nasir's suspected admirers into jail by the thousands; thus he made himself an open enemy, and had somehow to be countered. But this was difficult. Had he been just another reactionary, like King Husayn or Nuri al-Sa'id, he would have posed no serious threat to Nasir's moral prestige, and the line of counter-attack would have been clear and familiar. But of course he was no reactionary: he was a flaming radical, a hero to the slum-dwellers of Baghdad, the enemy of Nasir's presumed imperialist enemies and a friend of Nasir's presumed friend, the Soviet Union. Unlike domestic Arab Communists, Qasim showed signs of a certain mass appeal.

Because Qasim was the man he was, and followed the policy he did, he posed a threat to the integrity of the Syrian-Egyptian union. Syrians could not very well feel that he was conspiring with King Husayn or the Israelis or the American Central Intelligence Agency to undermine their nationalist virtue. They had joined the Egyptians partly for protection against the Baghdad monarchy; now the Baghdad monarchy was gone, and the need for protection with it. They had also joined Egypt in order to stimulate the overthrow of conservative regimes and bring such countries as Iraq into an Arab union. They could now see that the regime had indeed fallen, but that union was not the result. What, then, had they sacrificed their own independence for? What had the Ba'th sacrificed its formal existence for? If revolutionary Iraq would not join the union, who else ever would? By the logic of geography, history, economics, and social structure, Iraq was the country with whom Syria would have had natural cause to seek union in the first place, had it not been for the ideological unacceptability of the Hashimite regime. If the Syro-Egyptian union were to stop short of expansion, then Syrians must have second thoughts about its merits. The constitutional terms were tailored to Egyptian rather than Syrian preferences, and in any case the Egyptians outnumbered the Syrians five to one, and by sheer weight of numbers were bound to play a dominant role in the absence of any third partner.

Shifts in alignments

This situation placed 'Abd al-Nasir in a dilemma. He could not let Qasim's challenge go unanswered, when Iraqi jails were full of Nasirists, without a drastic loss of prestige. But to oppose Qasim effectively he had to adjust his stand towards other parties, for which he paid a price. He had to mend his relations with the Jordanian and Saudi Arabian governments in order to seek their co-operation in isolating Iraq within the Arab League: for, unsympathetic as they might be to a firebrand like Qasim, they had reason to relish the sight of Nasir in difficulty and could not be expected to go out of their way to help him fight his battles. In April 1959, at the meeting of the Council of the Arab League, the UAR sought but failed to obtain a formal condemnation of Qasim's government; for Jordan and Saudi Arabia were determined to enact a full price in the form of some kind of assurance of respect for the integrity and independence of their regimes. Somehow they appear to have obtained it, for Jordanian-UAR diplomatic relations were restored in August 1959, and two weeks later King Sa'ud was received in Egypt on an official visit.

Meanwhile 'Abd al-Nasir also mended his relations with the United States, whom he had so recently been confronting across the Lebanese frontier. In part this may have been done in deference to Amman and Riyad, but more especially it was a direct consequence of the rise of Communist activity in Iraq and of Nasir's sudden disenchantment with the Soviet Union. Communism, whether in Iraq or Syria (where the party continued its operations

c

underground) was not simply an ideology differing on this and that point from Nasir's brand of revolutionary nationalism, but something much worse: an organized movement in competition with his own, and outside his control. If the Soviets valued his friendship, it was up to them to restrain their Arab Communist clients.

This shift in alignments, modest though it was, caused dismay among the more militant pan-Arab enthusiasts inside and outside Syria, and especially among Ba'thists, who felt that 'Abd al-Nasir had compromised his revolutionary principles by consorting with reactionaries. If Qasim's parochialism and megalomania had robbed pan-Arabism of its opportunities in Iraq, so had Nasir's response robbed it in Jordan. The argument would have been lost on them—had any Arab leader had the courage to make it—that the UAR lacked the means to assure the future of Jordan against Israeli intervention if King Husayn were to be overthrown, and that thus the stationing of British troops in Jordan in July 1958 had averted a disaster for the UAR along with everyone else. Nasir's choices were limited by his dilemma; but for following the pragmatic rather than the doctrinaire path he was criticized for having deviated, as it were, from Nasirism.

Just before the Syrian secession, in the summer of 1961, the UAR government was placed in another version of essentially the same dilemma in the case of the Kuwait crisis. This oil-saturated principality, under British protection since 1899, was accorded full independence in mid-June 1961. Scarcely had the ink dried on the new Anglo-Kuwaiti treaty when Qasim, in his inimitable manner, announced that Kuwait was his southernmost province and that he and his army would liberate it at any moment. The Kuwaitis, with a per capita income slightly exceeding that of the United States, managed to conceal their desire for liberation, and the ruling

Shaikh promptly invoked the treaty and arranged for the arrival of a contingent of British troops to defend the territory.

In principle the UAR was devoted to the cause of unity, to terminating the privileged position of oil-rich monarchs (of whom the Shaikh of Kuwait happened to be the richest), and to a wider distribution and more constructive use of Arab oil revenues. The character of regimes aside, the union of Kuwait with Iraq made such economic sense; and as it happened, Iraq was a revolutionary and egalitarian republic, as was the UAR itself. But Qasim's Iraq was the UAR's sworn enemy, and to allow it any encouragement in this venture was unthinkable, especially when the UAR's own forward march had been stalled. Besides, the UAR's rediscovered diplomatic partners in Amman and Riyad sided unequivocally with the Shaikh of Kuwait as a matter of legitimist solidarity.

It was not difficult to justify opposition to Qasim's claim on Kuwait as such, on grounds of the principle of self-determination, which President 'Abd al-Nasir had often declared must be the basis of Arab unity. Iraq was mak'ng a bare-faced bid for annexation, and this was unacceptable. What was embarrassing was the spectacle of British troops camped on Arab soil, defending an interest which the UAR had declared as its own, at the invitation of the Kuwaiti government. When British forces had gone to Jordan in 1958, at least the UAR could feel free to denounce the operation without reserve, even while indirectly benefiting from it.

The difficulty was overcome, or at least minimized, by negotiating the replacement of the British force by a combined Saudi-Jordanian-UAR one. This was carried out on 14 September. But even then it did not enhance 'Abd Nasir's image for his troops to be seen, in the company of those of Sa'ud and Husayn, peacefully exchanging positions with Englishmen and continuing the defence of British imperial interests.

Syrian secession

After the departure of the Ba'th, 'Abd al-Nasir relied increasingly on Colonel Sarraj, who succeeded Hawrani as Chairman of the Syrian Provincial Council, to hold Syria together with his heavy-handed police methods. Meanwhile, proceeding in an opposite direction, Nasir sent his closest colleague, Marshal 'Abd al-Hakim 'Amir, to Syria as his special deputy, with instructions to brandish a carrot rather than a stick. This approach was particularly relevant to the spread of dissatisfaction within the Syrian army over such matters as the subordination of Syrian to Egyptian officers and the reduction of Syrian pay scales to Egyptian levels. But civilian grumbling over economic restrictions and increased duties on imported commodities also required his attention. There was nothing 'Amir could do about the drought that spoiled Syrian harvests for three consecutive years, though Nasir's prestige seemed somehow to suffer for it.

Nor was 'Amir's patience and goodwill any substitute for a real sense among the politically-minded Syrians of participating in the union as partners rather than poor relations, especially after the Ba'th had gone. Belatedly, in the summer of 1960, a National Assembly was called into being. But its members were directly appointed by presidential decree, not elected; and although a respectable number of members of the previous Syrian parliament and other notables were among them, they went off to sit in Cairo, whence they made little impression on the Syrian public. They were, of course, greatly outnumbered by their docile Egyptian colleagues; in Syria jokes began to circulate about the ineffectuality of the Assembly.

'You will find Syria a difficult country to govern', Shukri al-Quwatli is said to have told 'Abd al-Nasir. 'The Prophet himself travelled this far and turned back. Fifty per cent of the Syrians consider themselves national leaders, twenty-five per cent think they are prophets, and ten per cent imagine they are gods.' As time passed it seemed as if the identity of Syrian office-holders shifted gradually downwards from the gods and prophets to the mere leaders, and in the end to the remaining fifteen per cent who claimed no standing at all.

The lone remaining deity, 'Abd al-Hamid Sarraj, was removed from Syria in August 1961 and transplanted to Cairo as a Vice-President. A month later, chafing at his isolation and inactivity, he resigned and returned to Damascus. Later rumours circulated that he had started to plan a coup d'état. But in the event it was not Sarraj but other army officers with dissatisfactions of their own who on 28 September arrested Marshal 'Amir, put him on a plane bound to Cairo, and announced Syria's secession from the United Arab Republic.

We do not know precisely what was the nature of the conspiracy that arranged the coup, and what part civilians played in planning it. The Egyptian explanation, vehemently conveyed in a series of bitter speeches by President 'Abd al-Nasir and by the Cairo press and radio, was simple and, as far as it went, plausible enough: the union had been stabbed in the back by the Syrian wealthy class, the 'reactionaries', who had been affected by the programme of socialist legislation—nationalization of banks, insurance companies, and large-scale business and industrial corporations, as well as other measures—that Nasir had suddenly decreed in July 1961. These reactionaries, with help from the imperialists and reactionary Arab monarchs, had bribed and subverted an opportunistic clique of army officers to carry out the coup, in order that the *ancien régime* might be restored in Syria and the reforms of the unity period wiped out.

There was plenty of circumstantial evidence to support most of these charges. Certainly wealthy Syrians had been alienated, not only by the July 1961 measures but also by the extension of the Egyptian land reform to Syria in 1958 (and frequently carried out in an unscrupulous manner by Ba'th ministers) and by the imposition early in 1961 of severe currency exchange controls. Conservative Syrian politicians now promptly formed a government, held a parliamentary election in which they and their colleagues of the old school won the bulk of the seats, and then, early in 1962, repealed most of the nationalization decrees. The members of parliament took only two minutes' consideration to vote themselves a 333% rise in salary. While they did not repeal the land reform—presumably because they did not dare to do so—they managed to amend it, and there were complaints of landlords returning to their former properties, expelling occupants, and forcefully re-taking possession on the pretence that the reform had been abolished. If the wealthy classes had not made the coup, at least they took remarkable advantage of it.

Furthermore, because Jordan and Turkey both recognized the secessionist Syrian government with indecent haste and all the Great Powers soon followed suit, it seemed to some that at least the first two governments must have been privy to the plot. 'Abd al-Nasir lost no time in breaking off diplomatic relations with Amman and Ankara.

The underlying reasons

But to explain the Syrian secession in these terms and leave it at that was far too simple, and it carried unfortunate implications for Egypt's subsequent Arab policy.

Behind the stock expressions that were used to character-
ize the obstacles to Arab unity—*raj'iya* (reaction), *inti-
haziya* (opportunism), *iqlimiya* (provincialism)—lay a number of myths that the collapse of the union ought to have
exploded but in fact did not. One was that since all Arabs
are members of one 'nation', their diversities of geographi-
cal environment, spoken dialect, economic structure,
social tradition, and political experience and attitude are
in some sense artificial or at least of no more than incidental importance, and that concessions made to them are
therefore reprehensible. Another was that the needs and
desires of the mass of individual Arabs could really be
adequately understood and met within the confines of
simple ideological notions such as those shared by Nasirists and the Ba'th: liberation, unity, socialism, revolution.
Syrian army officers, for example, might be ready verbally
to endorse these things, but not necessarily ready to fight
for them in a given situation. To charge them with simple
opportunism on this account was not only unjust but,
what was more serious, signified the habitual inability of
those afflicted with ideological fixations to perceive or
accept the complications, ambiguities, tensions, rivalries,
contradictions, uncertainties, and contingencies that are
inherent in practical politics everywhere, even in those
societies which totalitarian regimes are purportedly pro-
pelling towards some kind of millennium.

It was not only the very rich, for instance, but also a
wide spectrum of lesser Syrian businessmen, extending
down to the shopkeeper level, who suffered to some degree
from the red tape and restrictions of economic and administrative reforms based largely on Egyptian rather than
Syrian needs. There were important reasons, having
nothing to do with the question of social oppression, why
economic reform aroused resentment in Syria. One was
that the administrative machinery of the Syrian govern-

ment was a rather simple affair by comparison to that of Egypt—scarcely worthy of a grocery shop, as Nasir once remarked.[7] Once a new set of import or currency or wage regulations was introduced, an extensive and hastily organized bureaucratic structure had to come into being. This in itself was bad enough in the eyes of individual Syrians, who were accustomed to dealing with government officials, to the extent that they did so at all, through familiar and often personally arranged channels; but it was made worse by the fact that Egyptian officials inevitably played a major role in establishing and administering the new procedures, since it was they who possessed the necessary experience. Consequently many ordinary Syrians now found it necessary to conduct business with unfamiliar and impersonal Egyptian bureaucrats and to follow the maddeningly complicated and interminable procedures for which the government of Egypt has long been famous.

To contain such dissatisfactions and enhance some feeling among Syrians that they contributed to the union and were not simply used by it, there was need for an indigenous political party or group of parties with their own organizational basis and their own means of dialogue with local popular opinion, independent of what the regime might see fit to bestow on them. This is not to say that Syria necessarily had to have a multi-party democracy, but simply that she needed to be governed in a manner that was institutionally geared to take some account of psychological and social realities. In comparison with Egyptians, Syrians are traditionally more diverse and vocal in their views, less amenable to authority, more jealous of their dignity, more accustomed to factional groupings, more excitable and less relaxed: in short, more difficult to govern in every way. The Ba'th, with its many faults, was

[7] *Mahadir jalsat mubahathat al-wahda* (minutes of the 1963 unity talks) (Cairo, 1963), p. 191.

at least a party with an acknowledged place on the Syrian political scene, composed of Syrians who were accustomed to dealing with other groups and taking the pulse of the various sections of the population, and led by men who enjoyed a certain personal prestige. The National Union, established in Syria as a replacement for political parties, lacked these advantages. It was too large, too diffuse, too anonymous in its composition, and too pretentious, monolithic, controlled from above, and ultimately irrelevant in the style and substance of its operations. It was all very well for Egyptian spokesmen to complain subsequently that the National Union had been infiltrated by reactionaries—that Dr Ma'mun Kuzbari, for instance, the first Prime Minister after the secession, had been chairman of the union's executive committee for the city of Damascus. But for one thing, conservative politicians had been tacitly encouraged to seek office in the National Union in 1959 at the expense of the Ba'th. For another, given the nature of the organization, it is hard to imagine how these men could have used their position in the union as any kind of springboard for the secessionist coup, or how for that matter they could be held responsible for the union's failure to amount to anything. The failure was not a matter of promoting socialist ideology, but of providing a field for effective political participation and expression of opinion, so as to take the edge off the widespread sense of disillusion among soldiers, political notables, businessmen, and ordinary citizens that made the secession possible.

Unfortunately, such practical lessons as these were not drawn in Cairo. It was curious that the Egyptian leaders, the erstwhile pragmatists who had been sceptical about rushing into union with Syria simply on the basis of nationalist fervour, and who had shown signs of distaste for the misty dogmatism of the Ba'th intellectuals, should now explain everything in equally abstract terms of a struggle between the forces of reaction and those of revolution in Arab society. Not only did the Egyptian government, immediately after the secession, adopt a repressive policy against its own upper class, sequestering their property, collectively branding them as 'enemies of the people', and putting some of them in jail; but also, in its relations with the rest of the Arab world, it reversed the course of moderation that it had cautiously developed since 1959 and assumed the stance of the militant revolutionary, uncompromisingly dedicated to the overthrow of all its conservative neighbours.

2

'Secessionism',
September 1961 - March 1963

*The differences now existing among certain Arab capitals
are natural in this stage of political and social revolution.
They do not prove that Arab unity is a myth. On the contrary, they are proof that this unity is real and genuine.*
MUHAMMAD HASANAYN HAYKAL, *al-Ahram*,
9 March 1962

FOR the ideologically conscious, the Syrian secession
mercifully cleared the air. Inter-Arab alignments now
took clear-cut form between the forces of good and evil,
with Revolution standing alone and defiant against Reaction. The years of the union had been marked by uncomfortable anomalies. If Arab union was the universal
will of the people, why were Syrian affairs such a per-
sistent problem for President 'Abd al-Nasir? And why had
he become so tolerant of Sa'ud and Husayn, to say nothing
of the prehistoric Imam of Yemen? Now these questions
no longer needed to be asked, for Cairo's reaction to the
secession was to declare political and diplomatic warfare
against the conservative regimes and to withdraw behind
the barricades of socialist reconstruction at home. The
picture continued to be complicated by the presence of
Qasim's peculiar regime in Baghdad. Yet even Qasim
could be conveniently classified in ideological terms: he
was a heretic, a deviationist.

In a fervent speech on 16 October President 'Abd al-
Nasir announced the main lines of Egypt's new ideological

and diplomatic position. 'We must have the courage to confess our errors', he said. 'We must blame ourselves for the collapse of the union with Syria.' Whatever fault attached to Egypt, Nasir manfully took on to his own shoulders. But what was the error to which, in Egypt's name, he confessed? It was that of 'compromising with the reactionaries', inside Syria and in inter-Arab affairs generally. He had now learned a good lesson: never to trust persons such as Kuzbari, Husayn, and Sa'ud, never to make allowances for their interests for the sake of solidarity and tolerance, never to imagine that the regeneration of the Arabs could be accomplished except by struggle and revolution. He had not opposed the secession with force because he was unwilling to shed Arab blood; but he would not abandon the 'noble Syrian people' whom the selfish secessionists had stabbed in the back, nor would Egypt abandon her Arab destiny and revert to isolationism. Meanwhile Egypt would continue to call herself 'the United Arab Republic'.

Thus, with his customary tactical skill, 'Abd al-Nasir responded to the disaster by seizing the psychological initiative and making a virtue of necessity. He made a show of strength of character by practising 'self-criticism', for which his supporters reverently commended him; but the nature of his 'confession' was such as to throw all moral responsibility on to his opponents. ('I confess that I was foolish enough to trust you.') He refused to recognize the new Syrian regime; he broke off diplomatic relations with Jordan; he terminated the loose confederation existing between the UAR and Yemen; he denounced the royal regime in Saudi Arabia. Thus he turned to his advantage the *Schadenfreude* of the rulers of these countries over the Syrian secession by denouncing them before they might see fit to denounce him, and by putting them on the defensive in the eyes of their own populations.

Egyptian reactions

Egypt's interest in the Kuwait affair also assumed a new light and 'Abd al-Nasir quickly withdrew his troops. It was now unthinkable for Egyptians to keep company with Syrian, Jordanian, and Saudi units; and in assailing the governments of these countries he had renounced all expectation of further co-operation from them against 'Abd al-Karim Qasim. As it happened, Qasim was at this moment in a state of high tension with the Iraq Petroleum Company, whose ownership overlapped with that of the Kuwait Oil Company. Perhaps the Egyptian withdrawal at this time would stimulate Qasim to reiterate his claims. If so, he would clash again with Jordan and Saudi Arabia, in which case a concerted partnership between them and Iraq against Egypt could be averted. As it turned out, Qasim made no new move toward Kuwait, but he did not drop his claims. In a gesture of supreme futility he recalled his ambassadors from countries in and out of the Middle East who had recognized Kuwait's independence; and from the moment the Arab League admitted Kuwait to membership, Iraq sulkily boycotted all further sessions. Egypt's tactical interests had been well served without cost to her revolutionary prestige.

By all these moves 'Abd al-Nasir restored to himself the ideological purity that Ba'thist and other radical critics had complained since 1959 that he had forfeited. Almost for the first time he could say to his supporters that his actions involved no concessions of principle and that he co-operated only with like-minded people. This position, despite or perhaps because of its isolation, recaptured for Nasir the high-pitched enthusiasm from his hard core supporters that had been his at Suez and at the birth of the UAR. But in 1961 he was much more alone than in 1956 or 1958.

Furthermore, while the Syrian coup aroused a considerable sentiment of isolationism and disillusion with pan-Arabism among politically sophisticated Egyptians, and thus threatened to undo all the efforts made by the regime since about 1954 to cultivate an Arab consciousness, 'Abd al-Nasir again sought to make the best of this by harnessing it to the image of revolutionary defiance. It was all the easier to stand proudly alone in the Arab world when many Egyptians had tired of Arab adventures and involvements. Both the convinced pan-Arabist and the convinced isolationist in Egypt could, each for the opposite reason, support the new policy—as long as it did not achieve concrete results.

Muhammad Hasanayn Haykal, the influential editor of *al-Ahram* newspaper, explained the UAR's new Arab policy by distinguishing between 'Egypt as a state' and 'Egypt as a revolution'.

As a state, Egypt deals with all Arab governments, whatever their forms or systems. She takes her place beside them in the Arab League and at the United Nations and concludes defence, trade, cultural, and other agreements with them. . . . As a revolution, Egypt should deal only with the people. This does not imply interference on our part in the affairs of others, since the fundamental premise of our struggle is that the Arab people are a single nation. If Egypt as a state recognizes frontiers in her dealings with governments, Egypt as a revolution should never hesitate or halt at frontiers, but should carry her message across them. . . . We have no right to separate ourselves from the struggle of other citizens of our nation. Egypt as a revolution will thus be not the Cairo government but a progressive party within the framework of the Arab nation. It should extend its hand to all progressive elements of the nation and openly stand beside them and support them. . . . We should do our utmost to co-operate with governments, but we should not extend such co-operation to the point where popular movements are affected. If the Arab League were to

be used to paralyse our movement, we should even be prepared
to freeze the operations of that body. We should also be prepared for a break in official relations with any Arab country
ruled by reaction if it should seek to pressure us into suspending
our legitimate appeal for freedom, socialism, and the unity of
all people of the Arab Nation.[1]

The shift was summed up by 'Abd al-Nasir himself in a
change of slogans. It had previously been customary to
speak of a 'unity of ranks' (*waḥdat al-saff*) among Arab
regimes of diverse internal orientation, in order better to
confront external dangers and pressures. 'Unity of ranks'
now gave way to the notion of 'unity of purpose' (*waḥdat
al-hadaf*). The new slogan was devised in response to
charges from Damascus, Amman, and Riyad that Nasir
was wrecking Arab solidarity. Nasir declared:

There are certain persons who today talk about the closing
of the Arab ranks. From the time of Nuri al-Sa'id they have
been talking about it. But what was the goal of such unity?
Was it to serve the interests of imperialism, or was it to serve
the interests of the Arab nation? Unanimity over purposes is
more important than unity of ranks. We call for unity of purpose, but we look with suspicion on slogans calling for unity of
ranks. Unity of ranks based on different purposes would drive
the entire Arab nation into danger. . . . It would mean we set
little store on our aspirations. . . . We seek to achieve unity
of purpose in the first place. Such unity can lead to unity of
ranks, because unity of purpose constitutes unity of all the Arab
peoples. All the Arab peoples have one and the same goal,
but certain rulers are working towards different goals. Therefore, they falsify the slogans and appeal for unity of ranks.[2]

Within this logic, it should be Egypt's policy not only
to acknowledge but even to project and sharpen the lack
of Arab solidarity.

[1] *al-Ahram*, 29 Dec. 1962.
[2] Speech of 22 Feb. 1962 (*President Gamal Abdel-Nasser's Speeches and Press-
Interviews, 1962*, pp. 29–30; trans. slightly adapted).

The United Arab Republic [wrote Haykal] should eschew such solidarity and keep its distance. With its faith in the inevitability of the Arab revolution . . . it should proclaim and persist in its difference. . . . By virtue of its historic situation, it is responsible for the Arab revolution and for Arab unity. It does not need to proclaim solidarity with certain rulers. It needs to stand sharply defined before all peoples. The extent of this sharp definition will be the extent of its success in Arab causes involving the entire nation.[3]

It may help put the implications of the above quotations in clearer perspective if we note their parallel with certain aspects of Leninist and Stalinist theory and practice—a source of inspiration, incidentally, of considerable importance for the leaders of the Egyptian revolution from about 1960 onward. First, there was the avowed rededication to domestic revolutionary goals after the Syrian secession, and minimization of diplomatic contact with neighbouring states, that characterized the early Stalinist phase of 'socialism in one country'. Internal developments in Egypt at this time underscored the parallel: consolidation of the massive nationalization of business promulgated in July 1961; a wave of arrests and property sequestrations carried out against the upper classes in October; a propaganda campaign against these classes as 'enemies of the people' and their formal exclusion from public life; the dissolution of parliament and of the National Union, both allegedly infiltrated by 'reactionaries', and a decision to replace the latter with a more tightly organized political movement called the Arab Socialist Union; and, in May 1962, the adoption of a 'Charter of National Action', or formal digest of revolutionary ideological principles.

Coupled with 'socialism in one country' was the counterpart of the Comintern of the 1930s implicit in the distinction between Egypt as a 'state' and a 'revolution', and

[3] *al-Ahram*, 9 Mar. 1962.

in Egypt's missionary vocation under the latter heading as the purveyor of revolution in disregard of state boundaries, as 'a progressive party within the framework of the Arab nation'. Egyptian policy, like that of the Soviet Union and other ideological regimes of the 1930s, would operate on two levels, each without acknowledgement of the other. ('This does not imply interference on our part in the affairs of others. . . .')

Thirdly, there is the sense of destiny, of historic inevitability, of unique moral responsibility and freedom from normal moral restraints, that special arrogance that afflicts crusaders for various causes once they become preoccupied with 'scientific' self-justification. Thus 'unity of purpose' in whatever terms 'Abd al-Nasir might conceive it could be assumed to 'constitute unity of all the Arab peoples', and the UAR, 'by virtue of its historic situation', could be thought to be 'responsible for the Arab revolution and for Arab unity'. The terminology of ideological pronouncements in Cairo by the end of 1961 had become replete with pseudo-Marxist references to 'inevitability', 'the elimination of social contradictions', 'scientific and revolutionary method', 'unity of struggle' against a host of evil forces (imperialism, Zionism, reaction, exploitation) which, 'despite apparent contradictions, have common aims and march in one procession directed by imperialism'.[4]

We are not concerned here to argue the question of the extent to which 'Abd al-Nasir's Arab Socialism is Marxist-Leninist, either in ideas or in practice. The point is simply that the ideological atmosphere in 1961–2 was marked by certain characteristics—revolutionary defiance and an urge to sanctify one's own expediency—that had become familiar to many Europeans a generation before. For com-

[4] Statement by the National Revolutionary Command of the Arab Socialist Ba'th Party (Rimawi splinter), Cairo 'Voice of the Arabs' Radio, 4 Jan. 1962.
D

mitted partisans of the UAR at the time, these qualities helped make everything seem wonderfully simple, and relieved their minds of the qualms of conscience that a serious interest in international affairs, with their shifting alignments and tactics, usually provokes. In time, of course, changing events were bound to reintroduce complications and complexes. But for the year and a half of the 'secessionist' period, diplomatic circumstances spared many pan-Arabists the need to make difficult choices of loyalty, while the explanations from Cairo spared them the need to make a painful re-examination of the premises of the pan-Arab movement. There was only one progressive force on the scene, and that was the UAR, surrounded by enemies; the fault in Syria had been that of the reactionaries; the march of history was on the side of the Revolution, and whatever practical encouragement it might be given was morally justified.

Even at the time when circumstances made this simple view most plausible, however, it seems doubtful that very many educated Egyptians considered the meaning of Syria's secession primarily in those terms, or that their leaders really expected them to do so. The pan-Arab idea in Egypt was still of very recent vintage, and the emotional commitment to it was shallow. 'Abd al-Nasir himself, in the 1963 unity talks, admitted that it was not until the time of Suez that Egyptians began to take Arabism seriously.[5] The anger in Egypt over the secession, which was genuine enough, emanated less from a concern for Arab unity or sense of kinship with Syrians than from a feeling of wounded pride, from the affront to that condescension and easy sense of superiority (not unlike the self-image conveyed by American use of the term 'leaders of the Free World') with which Egyptians had long been accustomed to regard the Asian Arab states. Some might

[5] *Mahadir*, p. 94.

sincerely regret the secession, others might feel a certain relief; but among both there seems to have been a strange combination of assumptions. The first was that the Syrian masses could not have wished to renounce the union, with all the benefits that Egypt had brought to it. The second was that the Syrians were an untrustworthy, ungrateful, disorderly, hot-headed and fickle lot who were unworthy of past or future Egyptian sacrifices. Few took seriously the propaganda references to 'the noble Syrian people'. At the same time it was hard for Egyptians of whatever shade of opinion to accept the idea that their country bore serious responsibility for the failure of the union through the overbearing ways of high and low ranking Egyptian personnel in Syria. For this accusation struck not so much at their government's policies as at their national character.

Practically speaking, the danger for Egypt's leaders was that politically conscious Egyptians would renounce their fragile interest in Arabism and lapse into an attitude of isolationism and indifference, rendering more difficult the policy of encouraging Arab solidarity under Egyptian leadership to which the regime had so deliberately attached importance since 1954. A constant theme in the President's speeches and in press editorials in the months after secession was the assertion that 'our Arabism is genuine and permanent'; so constant a theme, in fact, as to suggest strongly that many Egyptians needed convincing.

Thus the ideological picture that was painted in bold and simple strokes—the reactionary alliance pitted against the historic force of Arabism and socialism—was not simply a matter of dogmatic posturing, but rather reflected a tactical determination, always characteristic of the Egyptian leaders, to hold tenaciously to the initiative, to counter-attack whenever in danger of being out-manoeuvred and isolated within the Arab world. This had been their reaction to the Baghdad Pact, to the denial of Western arms and aid before Suez, to the Eisenhower Doctrine, to Qasim's separatism. The Syrian break-away was the most serious challenge of all, for it was a blow from within their acquired sphere, and deprived them of a base of support that they had depended and counted upon in their Arab policies ever since the beginning of 1955. It threatened to reduce to nothing the primary effort in foreign policy of the revolutionary regime since its beginning, namely to secure a firm and unchallengeable leadership among the Arab states with which it could confront the Great Powers in the jungle of world diplomacy. For if the loss of Syria had been met with anything less than a fierce counter-attack, Egypt would seem to be saying to herself and to other Arabs that she no longer took Arabism seriously.

Syrian reactions

The ideological campaign also helped to keep the Syrian secessionist authorities in a state of defensiveness and confusion. The Syrians found themselves constantly trying to prove their virtue, in terms of Arabism and socialism, in the face of Cairo's attacks. As far as Arabism was concerned, the presumptions were all against them, inasmuch as it was they themselves who had broken up the union. The word 'secessionist' (*infisali*) was made by Cairo propaganda to carry a treasonous connotation not unlike that of the word *shu'ubi* (defamatory of Arab virtues and pan-Arab solidarity) applied to Qasim and the Communists in Iraq. The Syrians adopted the name 'Syrian Arab Republic' for their resurrected state, and promptly circulated among the Arab governments a draft plan for federal union. They insisted that it was the Egyptians, and not they, who had shown themselves the enemies of unity by their domineering attitude, and that now the job of build-

ing a more solid unity would begin anew on better
foundations.

A manifesto supporting the secession was issued in
Damascus on 2 October bearing the signatures of eighteen
political leaders of diverse tendencies, including Khalid
al-'Azm, Sabri al-'Asali, and, most significantly, the Ba'th
leaders Akram Hawrani and Salah al-Din al-Bitar. (Later
Bitar was to regret this.) Michel 'Aflaq was out of the
country and therefore did not sign. Other politicians issued
their own declarations of support: Faris al-Khuri, Sultan
al-Atrash, and eventually Shukri al-Quwatli.

> Two happy dates have marked my life [said Quwatli],
> Syrian independence on 17 April 1946, and the Syrian
> Egyptian union of 5 February 1958. . . . I had hoped to share
> responsibility in the new state and contribute to drawing the
> other [Arab] peoples into the union, but I was greatly dis-
> appointed. . . . The Nasirite system relegated the majority of
> the population to the rank of traitors, governing by terror and
> trampling on the honour and dignity of citizens. . . . It gave
> the people a National Assembly whose sole function was to
> approve decisions coming from above. . . . They did not under-
> stand that what could be applied in Egypt could not be
> applied in Syria. . . . To maintain themselves they unleashed a
> class struggle.[6]

There were a good number of Syrians who had held high
civilian or military positions under the union, however,
who refused to condone the secession. Some were already
in Cairo; others fled there, to be put on pension by the
Egyptian government along with Iraqi and Jordanian
political exiles and to pass their time sitting in Lappas
Tea Room or at the Gezira Sporting Club.

It was even harder for the new Syrian government to
present themselves as progressives. They were mainly
members of the traditional Syrian political class, notables

[6] Quoted from *Cahiers de l'orient contemporain*, xlvii/4 (1961), p. 413.

of some landed and commercial wealth with local followings based on patronage and long-established family prestige. On 1 December a plebiscite was held on the new Syrian constitution, and simultaneously the voters cast ballots for members of the new parliament. The constitution was ratified by a 97.07 per cent majority, in the familiar manner of Middle Eastern plebiscites; this result was helped along by the procedure, in which voters applied for green slips of paper to place in the box, signifying 'yes', or red slips signifying 'no'. Meanwhile in the elections to parliament, candidates of the traditional class won about four-fifths of the seats. Party labels were prohibited in the campaign, but in practice the result was a come-back for the *laisser-faire* People's Party, which had suffered in the years before the union for the pro-Iraqi tendencies of many of its members. Their principal leader, Dr Nazim al-Qudsi, was now chosen by the parliament as President of the Republic and his colleague Dr Ma'ruf al-Dawalibi became Prime Minister. The new Speaker of Parliament was Ma'mun al-Kuzbari, who had been the first post-secession Prime Minister.

On 14 February the new parliament abolished the most important of 'Abd al-Nasir's July 1961 legislative decrees, under which all banks and insurance companies and numerous other enterprises had been nationalized, and individuals had been forbidden to own a total of more than £S100,000 (about £10,000) in other firms. These properties were now de-nationalized and a very much milder Industrial Organization Law was passed instead. The main provision was to impose moderate restrictions on the concentration of ownership: founders' shares of new companies were limited to 40 per cent, and in the case of companies over ten years old, individuals were restricted to a maximum stock ownership of £S175,000 *per company*. Modest provision was made for the sale of stock to workers.

The Minister of National Economy, 'Adnan al-Quwatli, explained that the 1961 legislation had consisted of

improvisations made for propaganda purposes. They were not in the interest of the worker, and denied all his gains; nor were they in the interest of the national economy, for they prevented its progress and prosperity. . . . [They] aimed not at economic or social reform, but at enabling the rulers to dominate the people and their livelihood in a direct manner without encouraging the citizens to establish prosperous industries and without founding a just social relationship between the worker and employer. This was particularly because the previous laws killed individual initiative and private efforts and crushed every notion of establishing projects or expanding industrial activity. . . .

It thus becomes indisputably clear that the new law is the one which gives concrete form to the idea of constructive socialism and establishes genuine social justice, contrary to the stipulations of the previous laws of improvisation and empty propaganda.[7]

President 'Abd al-Nasir retorted with a scornful reference to 'the capitalists and monopolists who speak of socialism' and to an article in the Damascus press calling for a socialist programme similar to that of the British Conservative Party.[8]

Inasmuch as the Syrian secessionist leaders felt compelled to cling to such slogans as Arab unity and socialism —slogans which had become closely bound up with 'Abd al-Nasir's name in the minds of so many Arabs—it was clear that they were conducting their struggle with Cairo under a grave handicap. The parliamentary elections, by which they had hoped to consolidate their legitimacy, had been of little help. Nasir had vowed just after the secession that he would not treat with a regime in Damas-

[7] Damascus Radio Domestic Service, 15 Feb. 1962.
[8] Speech of 22 Feb. 1962 (*Nasser's Speeches, 1962*, p. 33; trans. slightly adapted).

cus that was not representative of the people; now he had only to point to the complexion of the new parliament and its legislative programme, and maintain his aloofness. For another year a succession of Syrian cabinets floundered in desperation and insecurity as they sought to shore up their position by improvising domestic and foreign policies in which they themselves did not believe.

The Ba'th split

Amidst these developments the Ba'th Party was in an increasingly uncomfortable position. As its leaders had left office long before the secession, they bore no responsibility for the unpopular July 1961 decrees; nor had they played any discernible role in the secession itself. But Hawrani and Bitar had subsequently put their names to the secession manifesto, and a large number of followers left the party in protest.

In the ensuing parliamentary elections Hawrani won a seat, but Bitar lost. In parliament Hawrani bitterly denounced the emasculation of 'Abd al-Nasir's social legislation, but he was at one with the conservative government leaders in castigating Nasir himself, in loudly voicing his satisfaction at the termination of Nasir's 'dictatorship', and in charging that Nasir had abandoned the Arab cause in Palestine and sold himself to the United States in return for economic aid.

The 'Aflaq–Bitar wing of the party were as dismayed as Hawrani at the reactionary tendencies of the secessionist government, but—perhaps because they lacked Hawrani's extraordinary knack for tactical flexibility and unconcern for the consistency of his positions—they drew the conclusion that they should avoid any appearance of being associated with it. Also, the uninhibited way in which both Hawrani and the 'reactionaries' rejoiced in the break-up of the union and vilified President 'Abd al-

Nasir (whom the party had hitherto avoided criticizing by name) was unseemly and embarrassing. Bitar repudiated his signature of the manifesto; he and 'Aflaq and their friends chose to wait quietly, keep their hands clean, and ride out the storm of 'reactionary secessionism'. Hawrani's instinct, by contrast, was to try to make the most of it.

In time the two wings of the party drifted apart. On 18 June Hawrani issued a statement announcing that he was forming a new party of his own, and the next day Michel 'Aflaq declared that Hawrani and his followers had been expelled, and that the decision had in fact been taken at a party congress the previous month in Beirut. Thus ended the alliance that Hawrani had made with 'Aflaq and Bitar in 1952. During the remainder of the 'secessionist' period in Damascus, Hawrani himself remained in the wings but several of his associates served as cabinet ministers under successive prime ministers. Towards the end, in February 1963, Hawrani negotiated a 'national pact' with the Prime Minister Khalid al-'Azm and the Muslim Brotherhood leader 'Isam al-'Attar—men for whom he would have had little use at an earlier stage in his career. 'Aflaq and Bitar he dismissed as 'Nasirite agents'.

Other divisions meanwhile emerged between the conservative political group controlling the government and a large section of the army officer corps, from among whose ranks the secession had been engineered. On the whole the officers tended to much more leftist political and social ideas than the politicians. Military support for secession was not based on anger over nationalizations or land reform, or even over Egyptian political domination, but mainly on the irritation felt by Syrian officers at the blows that their self-respect had suffered under Egyptian command. Indeed, the gestures made by the politicians in the name of Arabism and socialism were presumably meant to placate opinion within the Syrian army as much as within the general public. A good many officers with strong Nasirite sympathies, notably in the Aleppo and Homs regions, had been powerless to prevent the secession but none the less remained in their positions; others, while accepting the break, did so with some reluctance and desired to follow Egyptian leads in foreign and domestic policy as closely as possible. Colonel Haydar al-Kuzbari, a relative of Ma'mun al-Kuzbari, one of the master-minds of the coup and known for his conservative political views, was arrested and jailed a few weeks after the secession.

The 'Azma government

On 28 March 1962 the army high command moved against the civilian regime it had itself brought to power. President Qudsi, all but one of the cabinet ministers, and a good many members of parliament were arrested. They were charged with abusing their mandate, indulging in the spoils of office, and failing to work effectively for Arab unity. Great confusion followed. The officers were deeply divided among themselves, and a faction in Aleppo seized the opportunity to proclaim their will to reunite Syria with Egypt, hoping perhaps for Egyptian intervention. As this did not materialize they were forced after a few days to hand over control to a force sent from Damascus; a number of Nasirite officers fled; order was restored, and a settlement was negotiated between army factions under which half a dozen officers of antagonistic tendencies were exiled to Europe. The explanation of these events remained shrouded in mystery, but it became clear that the principal officers in the army had been guilty of gross political incompetence, for they were not only at odds with one another but were also unable to find a respectable body of civilians to form a new government on their behalf.

At length they were driven to the humiliation of releasing those under arrest and asking President Qudsi to return to office. Parliament was formally dissolved and the Dawalibi cabinet replaced by one under Dr Bashir al-'Azma, who was known for his more progressive outlook and who had held office under the union with Egypt. The new government was cautiously welcomed in Cairo. It made a number of moves calculated further to placate Nasirite sentiment. The Khumasiya Company, the largest industrial combine, was re-nationalized; previous amendments to the 1958 agrarian reform legislation were repealed. The government declared that it would work towards union with the 'liberated' Arab countries, particularly 'dear Egypt' and 'sisterly Iraq'—thus pretending to overlook the fact that Egypt and Iraq were scarcely on speaking terms, but implying at least a loosening of its relations with 'Abd al-Nasir's reactionary arch-enemies, Saudi Arabia and Jordan. A large committee of political figures, but so diverse in its composition as to guarantee ineffectiveness, was appointed to formulate recommendations on steps to Arab unity. Dr 'Azma made the further gesture of saying that President 'Abd al-Nasir had been 'stabbed in the back by Syria's secession'.

These steps, while shifting Syria's official stance somewhat in the direction of Cairo, were much too equivocal to placate the Egyptian regime. After a brief period of reserved silence, the Cairo press and radio denounced the 'Azma government as being little better than its predecessor, and charged it with being under the nefarious influence of Akram Hawrani. Before long the 'Azma government took to answering the Egyptian attacks, and complained in particular of alleged attempts at sabotage and subversion by Egyptian agents infiltrating into Syria through Lebanon.

These complaints led to a violent confrontation at a meeting of the Arab League Council at the end of August, at the Lebanese town of Shtura, which brought the already moribund League virtually to the point of collapse. In a well-calculated needling gesture the UAR pointedly sent as its delegation a group of three Syrians who had settled in Cairo after September 1961 in protest against the secession, headed by the former army colonel and cabinet minister Akram Dayri. The Syrian delegates, for their part, distributed copies of a 'Black Book' that presented a detailed exposé of sins committed by the authorities during the union. Syria now entered charges of Egyptian interference and incitement. The UAR in turn accused the Damascus government of conducting a 'torture campaign against nationalist elements in Syria' and serving the purposes of imperialism. Then the Syrians charged that the UAR was working secretly with the United States to shelve the Palestine question, and produced the photostat of a reputed circular from the Foreign Ministry in Cairo to its diplomats abroad, instructing them to be 'non-committal' in statements regarding Palestine so as to 'facilitate negotiations' with the United States.

Impotence of the Arab League

This was the cue for the UAR delegation to stalk out of the Shtura meeting in protest against the Syrian government's 'slander'. 'The Arab League', said Dayri, 'has become a humiliation to its member states. It can do nothing for the aspirations of the Arab struggle.' 'Abd al-Khaliq Hassuna, the Egyptian Secretary-General of the Arab League, broke down in tears. The remaining delegations, embarrassed by the whole affair, voted ten to Syria's one that the Council 'could not continue discussion of the Syrian complaint against UAR interference in Syria's affairs because the UAR had withdrawn.' The Egyptian government thenceforth ignored the Arab League for over a year. (The Iraqi government, still brooding over Kuwait, had not attended the Shtura meeting.)

Other signs of the League's impotence followed. One was its inability to play any useful role in the conflict over the civil war in Yemen, which broke out in September 1962 and into which Egypt, Saudi Arabia, and Jordan were soon drawn. Another, which once again pitted Egypt against Syria, was a dispute over the dismissal of the Commissioner of the Arab League Office for the Boycott of Israel, in January 1963. The Commissioner, Dr 'Abd al-Karim al-'Aidi, and the permanent headquarters were located in Damascus. Dr 'Aidi, who had held his post since 1950, was the one Syrian of high rank on the League staff. He had incurred Egyptian displeasure in September 1962 by seeing fit to receive certain documents, presented to him in his capacity as the ranking representative of the League in Damascus, from the Egyptian military attaché in Beirut who had defected and taken asylum in Syria. Possibly acting under pressure from the Egyptian government, the Secretary-General, Hassuna, relieved 'Aidi of his post on the pretext that 'Aidi had passed the retirement age of 60, and appointed in his place an Egyptian, Muhammad Mahgub. The Damascus government took this as a direct challenge. With support from Jordan, Saudi Arabia, and Iraq, it refused to recognize the legality of Mahgub's appointment and established a 'regional' boycott office in Damascus under its own authority. It maintained that 'Aidi had been appointed by a vote of the League Council and could only be dismissed and replaced by the same body.

By the end of January 1963, then, members of the League

had fallen into a long and complex pattern of quarrels. Iraq refused to recognize Kuwait, and on this account had recalled its ambassadors from all other League members. Egypt had never recognized the Syrian regime, and had broken off diplomatic relations with Jordan. After the Yemeni republican revolution, diplomatic relations between Saudi Arabia and Egypt were broken off as well. Egypt, Iraq, Syria, and Lebanon recognized the Yemeni republicans; Saudi Arabia and Jordan still recognized the royalists. Syrian-Lebanese relations had been spoiled as a by-product of the Syrian-Egyptian confrontation, and the frontier was closed. Commenting on the Boycott Office dispute, a Lebanese journalist remarked that 'Israel can henceforth have the moral satisfaction of no longer being the country placed under the ban of the organization formed by her neighbours, but simply one of the countries of this region that boycott each other'.[9]

None of this mattered to the Egyptian President. He had decided, in the autumn of 1961, to build his policy on the foundation of revolutionary ideology so as to stimulate internal pressure on his rivals. Not only did he not seek co-operation from the Syrian, Iraqi, Jordanian, and Saudi governments, but he spurned it as a liability. The Yemeni revolution initially seemed to him a golden opportunity: his army intervened as the champion of revolutionary progress, while Saudi Arabia and Jordan, who felt compelled to support the royalists out of dynastic solidarity, were put in an ultra-reactionary light in the eyes of their own peoples. Both Syria and Iraq also recognized the revolutionaries, but could exert no influence on Yemen and could take no credit; and in the case of Syria, her conservative leaders were in the particularly awkward position of striving to cultivate a 'progressive' posture over the Yemen affair, in pursuit of the will-o'-the-wisp of

[9] René Aggiouri in *L'Orient* (Beirut), 25 Jan. 1963.

domestic popular support, while having to condone the principle of massive Egyptian intervention in the internal politics of a fellow Arab state (against which, in their own case, they had just finished complaining at Shtura) and running counter to the interests of the Saudi and Jordanian governments on which they otherwise relied for support. It was a splendid manifestation of the Syrian government's miserable dilemma, that of having to resist the Egyptian revolutionary challenge, in defence of her own conservative interests, by making half-hearted and unconvincing revolutionary gestures.

Iraqi and Syrian coups d'état

The final phase in this demoralizing process came with the Iraqi coup d'état of 8 February 1963, which eliminated Qasim and his regime and brought to power the Iraqi branch of the Ba'th Party. The Egyptians hailed the overthrow of their hated rival and the advent of a regime pledged to pan-Arab and socialist goals. An Iraqi delegation triumphantly flew to Cairo and attended the Arab Unity Day ceremonies on 22 February (marking the anniversary of the formation of the UAR) at 'Abd al-Nasir's side. While Nasir had had his problems with the Syrian Ba'thists during the union, the Iraqis were a fresh group of persons of whom he had no bad memories, and who now declared themselves eager to co-operate with him. He recognized, in any case, that for the moment they were the only organized Arab force in Iraq surviving four and a half years of Qasim and the Communists; and besides, they had installed as titular head of state the man who had been his principal champion in Iraq in 1958, 'Abd al-Salam 'Arif.

What was good news for 'Abd al-Nasir was naturally bad news for the Syrian government. They had, as it happened, been recently engaged in solidifying their relations with Qasim. They were also in the midst of important negotiations for economic aid agreements with the Soviet Union and China, both of whom were now furious over the mass killings and arrests of Iraqi Communists by the new regime in Baghdad. The Ba'th Party had its centre in Damascus, where its Secretary-General, Michel 'Aflaq, made his headquarters, and presumably the Iraqis would be responsive to him and other Syrian members of the party's 'national' (i.e. pan-Arab) council. We have seen that the Syrian Ba'th, having rid themselves of Akram Hawrani and his followers, had held aloof from the Damascus government and withheld their support, refusing to associate themselves with its hostility to Nasir and its conservative domestic policies.

Yet the government, hard pressed to gain the tolerance of 'progressive' and pan-Arab elements if it could not have their positive co-operation, had felt unable to suppress Ba'thist activity. After the Iraqi coup Michel 'Aflaq was allowed to travel freely between Damascus and Baghdad, holding long consultations with his Iraqi colleagues and issuing enthusiastic statements to the press in support of them. The government itself, trying to regain some semblance of initiative, made its own overtures to Baghdad for the negotiation of a Syro-Iraqi union. As on so many other occasions of Syrian appeals for union, this one was simply a reflection of her own weakness. Just as in 1958 an insecure Syrian government had appealed to Egypt to save her from Iraq, now another one was appealing to Iraq against Egypt. But the Iraqis were not interested in dealing with the existing Syrian regime: they were waiting for another one, and meanwhile they were holding talks with 'Abd al-Nasir.

The Syrian coup came exactly a month after the Iraqi one, on 8 March. Unlike that of Iraq, it was carried out almost effortlessly, and without violence. The secessionist regime had become too demoralized to resist. The year and a half since secession had been punctuated with repeated schisms and quarrels among civilian politicians and within the army command. There had been four cabinets in seventeen months, and the last one, that of Khalid al-'Azm, was casting about for fresh support when the coup put it out of its misery. General Zahr al-Din, the army commander, Akram Hawrani, and President Qudsi were arrested; Khalid al-'Azm quietly went home to his flat upstairs in the Turkish Embassy and remained there for many months under cover of the embassy's diplomatic immunity.[10]

As in Iraq, a National Revolutionary Command Council (NRCC) of anonymous officers and civilians assumed sovereign power and appointed a Ba'th-led cabinet of ministers; Salah al-Din Bitar became Premier. The Council announced that they had taken power in order to atone for the 'crime' of secession and to lead Syria back to union, this time with both Egypt and Iraq. 'Abd al-Nasir immediately cabled his congratulations and, for the first time since the separation, extended diplomatic recognition to an independent Syria; his picture triumphantly reappeared in the streets and windows of Damascus and Aleppo. His refusal to compromise with reactionaries and separatists in the Arab world had seemingly been vindicated, and the road to a revived and expanded Arab union was open.

[10] The building belonged to 'Azm, and the Embassy was his tenant. After the coup, to cover himself legally, 'Azm 'rented' his own flat to the Embassy but continued to live there.

3

The Cairo Negotiations,
March - April 1963

We are really suffering from a complex about union because of too much talk.

GAMAL 'ABD AL-NASIR to the Syrian and Iraqi delegations in Cairo, 14 March 1963

THE 8 March coup was not exactly Ba'thist. It was led by Major-General Ziyad al-Hariri, an independent-minded and reputedly ambitious officer who had been serving as commander on the Syrian-Israeli armistice line. Hariri had no party connexions; some Ba'thists were inclined to criticize him for having served the secessionist regime in a responsible position. Originally associated with him in laying the plot were two other unaffiliated officers: Rashid Qutayni, Chief of Military Intelligence, and Muhammad al-Sufi, a high-ranking member of GHQ. The coup was planned for 7 March, and the leaders of the various pan-Arabist political parties—the Ba'th and others—were discreetly informed. Qutayni and Sufi withdrew from the plot at the last moment, claiming that word of it had leaked to the government, and so the unionist politicians were advised that plans were cancelled; but Hariri then decided to act on his own, on 8 March. He informed the Ba'th of this, and secured the assistance of some of their officer partisans, but he said nothing to the other parties, probably out of fear that their army connexions would lead back to Sufi and Qutayni.

Thus it was that by accidental circumstance, when the

coup came on 8 March, the Ba'th were on hand to assist and take credit for it. Salah Bitar and other Ba'thists were quickly summoned to form a government. Sufi and Qutayni were awakened from their beds, the one to be made Minister of Defence and the other Deputy Chief of Staff.

The new Syrian regime

The principal officers in the coup, casting about for a figure of suitable stature to preside over their Revolutionary Council, settled on a mild-mannered and relatively inexperienced young man, Colonel Luay al-Atasi. Atasi had spent five years in Egypt, first as assistant military attaché and then, during most of the union, with a unit in Alexandria. After a brief tour of duty in the UAR Embassy in Moscow he had returned to Syria in October 1961 and was on hand to play a leading role in the army uprising at Aleppo the next March. For this he was later interned in Mazza Prison until the 8 March coup. Now he was summoned from prison, made a lieutenant-general, and elected President of the NRCC. Though not a Ba'thist, Atasi had many friends in the party and was regarded as sympathetic to it; but it appears that he was chosen to lead the NRCC not for his party connexions but for the respect he had earned among all army factions by his conduct at Aleppo. It is curious that another man who is said to have been considered for the presidency of the NRCC, Brigadier Amin al-Hafiz, was unofficially a Ba'thist but, as in Atasi's case, was put forward by reason of his personal reputation for honesty and straightforwardness. After serving as army commander at Deir ez-Zor and then as an instructor at the Military College, he had been relegated by the secessionist government to what must surely be the world's most useless sinecure, the post of

Syrian military attaché in Buenos Aires. Hafiz was a much more intelligent and decisive person than Atasi, but perhaps at the time that was a liability, in view of his party attachment; and besides, he was in Argentina. Instead he was made Minister of the Interior. Within a few months he was to become dictator of Syria.

Bitar's cabinet was formed with a hard core of Ba'thist membership but with half the places allotted to independents and to leading members of the other Arab unionist organizations. These latter were notified of the coup they thought had been called off and invited to join the government: Nihad al-Qasim of the United Arab Front, who became Deputy Prime Minister; Sami Sufan of the Socialist Unity Movement; and Hani al-Hindi and Jihad Dahi of the Arab Nationalist Movement.

Individually, each of these three parties was easily outclassed by the Ba'th in organizational strength, military following, and public reputation. Their leaders were relatively unknown. Nihad al-Qasim had served as Minister of Justice for Syria for a time during the union, but had no great following. The Arab Nationalist Movement was largely composed of university students and young graduates, especially (as in Hindi's case) from the American University of Beirut where the organization had first come into being. The ANM had the advantage of being widely organized, if not thickly populated, in semi-secret units throughout the cities of Lebanon, Syria, Jordan, and Iraq, in a manner comparable to that of the Ba'th; and during the union, while the Ba'th underwent a strained relationship with President 'Abd al-Nasir, the ANM had acquired a reputation as 'Abd al-Nasir's most loyal supporters (or, in Ba'thist eyes, stooges). On the other hand the ANM had developed little interest in socialism, or in any other ideology other than that of Arab unity itself. Nasir's own turn to the left in July 1961 and the rapid acceleration of his doctrinal consciousness after that time had left many ANM members far behind, and as late as 1964 it was to remain a cause of some debate within the ranks of the Movement to what extent they should follow the Leader in this path.

Of the three non-Ba'th parties Sami Sufan's Socialist Unity Movement probably possessed the largest membership. The SUM consisted of former members of the Ba'th itself, who had split off after September 1961 in protest against Hawrani's and Bitar's signature of the secession manifesto. Despite this legacy of ill feeling, in March 1963 it was they who were potentially most sympathetic to co-operation with the Ba'th. Hawrani had been expelled from the party, and it was known that Bitar had come to regret his initial endorsement of the secession. Now that this incident had lost its significance and the Ba'th were once again championing the cause of Arab unity, the ideological orientation that they and the SUM shared in common seemed a promising basis for renewed co-operation. But dealings between them would not be on equal terms: neither the SUM nor Sami Sufan were names that many Syrians could recognize, at a time when Michel 'Aflaq and Salah al-Din Bitar had been building their reputations, and their movement, for twenty years.

None the less, if these three parties individually were of secondary account, collectively it was inconceivable that the Ba'th should begin its period of rule by ignoring them, despite its own illusions of destiny. One reason we have already alluded to: the officer corps was not wholly or even predominantly Ba'thist, nor were all the officers who had made the coup. For non-Ba'th officers, whether Nasirist or not, only a coalition government could offer any assurance against politically motivated purges and transfers at their expense. A broader consideration was the prospect of dealing with 'Abd al-Nasir. Given their

background and conditioning, it was almost by reflex that
the Ba'th should make Arab unity their first item of business, even if their own Syrian house cried out to be put in
order. The presence of the month-old Ba'thist regime in
Baghdad strengthened the temptation to plunge into the
game of unity—partly because a Ba'thist Iraq and a
Ba'thist Syria could easily negotiate union with each other,
and partly because Iraq seemed a heaven-sent bargaining
partner with which to confront 'Abd al-Nasir. For they
would certainly have to confront him. An Iraqi-Syrian
union without recourse to the Egyptians would suffer in
pan-Arab eyes from a gross lack of legitimacy and would
be for ever vulnerable to Egyptian criticism and harassment. The 1958–61 union had demonstrated that Nasir's
personality was not enough on which to build a union,
but the secessionist period had shown how little could be
done without his tolerance. In any case, the Ba'th's own
doctrinal instincts led them to reopen the subject of
Egyptian-Syrian unity. This time, with Iraqi participation they could hope to do so on their own terms. But if
they were to treat with 'Abd al-Nasir, they must treat also
with his Syrian followers, as a sign of their sincerity—or,
to put it differently, as a gesture of respect for the complex which the Egyptian leader had developed since September 1961 over his erstwhile Northern Province.

Thus the Ba'th, impelled by reputation and mentality
to fasten their attention on inter-Arab affairs before the
dust had settled in Damascus, began with a relationship
with the other three unionist parties that was bound to
lead into contradictions. They sought to grant these parties
a role sufficient to enable themselves to negotiate with
'Abd al-Nasir, but not enough to jeopardize their own
control—either of the course of the negotiations or of the
political scene at home. But the other parties had their
own strong convictions about Arab unity. They saw Nasir

—not the Ba'th—as the instrument of destiny. They wanted terms that would promote his influence and enhance his prestige (and with it, locally, their own). Once they were participants in the Syrian government they were naturally even more eager to fly to Cairo than the Ba'th, for their purposes were free of ambiguity. The Ba'th could not allow themselves to be outbid in enthusiasm for union; they could not do without these partners; but nor could they' accede to the kind of union the partners preferred, which was summed up in the slogan 'A return to 27 September'. In the end they would have to clash with the Nasirites, who would not remain satisfied with a minor role, and consequently with 'Abd al-Nasir himself. Five months later, after the clash with Nasir had come and the illusion of Arab unity had been shattered, the Ba'th were to complain that his demanding attitude had cost Syria precious time that could have been more fruitfully devoted to domestic progress.[1] But it was they who had initiated the Cairo negotiations in the first place. It was their own ideologically motivated compulsion to ignore domestic affairs (except the elimination of their rivals) and to stumble into an absurd venture for unity with a man they distrusted, and seeking terms that he was bound to refuse, that had brought about the struggle.

The 1963 unity talks

The text of the Cairo unity discussions of March and April 1963, subsequently published by the Egyptian authorities,[2] is a fascinating political document of first-class

[1] *al-Ba'th* newspaper, 4 Aug. 1963.

[2] The transcript was printed in instalments in *al-Ahram* newspaper and broadcast over Cairo Radio from 21 June to 22 July 1963, and later published in book form under the title *Mahadir jalsat mubahathat al-wahda* (see p. vii above). Translations of the Cairo Radio broadcasts of the transcript, which the author has not seen, are available in the BBC *Summary of World Broadcasts*, Part IV, for the above-mentioned period. A more accessible and

importance to all those interested in Arab affairs. Ostensibly the talks were held in order to negotiate a Syrian-Egyptian-Iraqi federal union, but the larger part of them was devoted not to bargaining but to other things: notably to informal, very personal discussions between President 'Abd al-Nasir and the leading Syrian Ba'thists—Bitar, 'Aflaq, and 'Abd al-Karim Zuhur—of their past dealings with each other during the 1958–61 union, of the current situation in Syria, and of their ideological approach to such questions as democracy, socialism, and party organization. The talks are also interesting for the light they shed on the personalities of the participants and, of course, for all that they reveal of the course and tenor of the negotiations themselves.

The talks were held in three stages: five Syrian-Egyptian-Iraqi meetings from 14 to 16 March; five bilateral Syrian-Egyptian meetings on 19 and 20 March; and finally, ten meetings from 6 to 14 April, of which the first two sessions were between Egypt and Syria only, and the last eight between all three countries once more. But for the purposes of our discussion here it is easier to divide the record of the talks into two parts: first, the airing of complaints between 'Abd al-Nasir and the Syrian Ba'th, until 7 April; second, the trilateral negotiations for a federal union, from 7 to 14 April. Although two of the leading Iraqi Ba'thists—'Ali Salih al-Sa'di and Talib Husayn Shabib—were present at the first round of talks, the conversation centered on Syria, with the Iraqis intervening only intermittently to support the Syrian Ba'th's positions.

The extent to which the published document is accurate

---

readable, but considerably abridged translation is in the American University of Beirut's *Arab Political Documents, 1963* (see above, p. vii). In the following pages all quotations from the unity talks are from the latter source, referred to as *APD*, unless otherwise indicated.

and complete cannot be determined with any assurance. Subsequently the Syrians claimed that the Egyptians had doctored the transcript in such a manner that 'Abd al-Nasir's views were clearly set out while the Syrian statements were 'plucked' so that 'one would imagine these conversations to be a debate between two deaf men'.[3] The Iraqis also challenged the accuracy of certain passages, alleging both fabrications and omissions. But neither the Iraqi nor the Syrian delegation possessed its own record, and consequently, apart from occasional items, they were unable to present much of a case. At the first meeting, on discovering that the talks were to be tape-recorded, they obtained assurance (so they later said) that copies of the transcript would regularly be given them for correction and approval, but this assurance was not honoured. Salah al-Din Bitar stated categorically to the author that the second round of talks, of which the published record put him and 'Aflaq in a particularly bad light, was not recorded by any visible device, nor was a secretary present to take notes. General Luay al-Atasi, however, recalled the presence of a secretary in both the second and third rounds. Possibly a recorder was concealed. It should also be noted that the version broadcast on Cairo Radio was not a playback of the original but was read from a script. Rather remarkably, Bitar insisted to the author that he had never read the published version. After questioning both Bitar and, more especially, Talib Shabib in detail about the various stages of the negotiations, the author concluded that there was at least a large body of the published record that was substantially accurate. The exact wording of the text in any given passage, however, should be regarded with caution; and it is with this reservation that we proceed to discuss the published minutes of the talks.

[3] *al-Ba'ath*, 4 July 1963.

Syrian-Egyptian-Iraqi meetings

In the opening meeting 'Abd al-Nasir threw both the
Syrian and Iraqi Ba'thists off their guard. They had come
in search of a quick agreement and to ask for his terms.
He replied, in effect, that he was in no hurry and that they
would have to wait until he had obtained satisfaction on a
long list of preliminary questions from the Syrians. It was
necessary to clear the air, and then one would see what
might be done. He was willing to consider another union
with a representative Syrian government, but not simply
with the Ba'th, in whom he had no confidence. The record
of the previous union must be examined. What had been
its lessons? Who was now governing Syria, and with
whom was he being asked to negotiate? What were the
Ba'th's views on the organization and programme of a
future union?

In the abstract these seem to have been reasonable
questions. 'We will tell you our complaints about the past',
said 'Abd al-Nasir in effect, 'and you must tell us yours. We
shall practise self-criticism. We will explain our ideology
to you, and you explain yours. Then we can compare our
proposals for the future.'

But in fact 'Abd al-Nasir put his questions in a heavily
loaded manner that struck at the very basis of the Ba'th's
dignity and could only discomfit their representative at the
talks, 'Abd al-Karim Zuhur, who would much have preferred to let bygones be bygones. For Nasir summarized
his own views by saying that he regarded the Ba'th's past
performance as deceitful and opportunistic. In particular
he claimed that the collective resignation of Ba'th ministers
in December 1959 as a withdrawal from the union itself,
'as a crime', a 'stab in the back', and that Hawrani and
Bitar, in signing the secession manifesto of 1961, had
signed the union's death warrant. Furthermore, he doubted

that the Ba'th, despite their intellectual pretensions, had any clear ideological principles other than a lust for power. Why did they want a tripartite unity? Was it in order to outvote Egypt and place 'Abd al-Nasir 'between the hammer and the anvil'? If so, he would have no part in it.[4]

Thus 'Abd al-Nasir made it plain that negotiations could proceed only if the Ba'th in Syria (and, presumably, Iraq) renounced all hopes of preponderance in the government, confessed its past sins, and looked to Egypt's much-vaunted Charter of National Action and to Egypt's revolutionary experience for inspiration. One could only suppose that if the Ba'th conceded this much, they would also find themselves compelled to follow the Egyptian lead in planning for the future. The Ba'th must come to Nasir as his clients; he would not unite at their convenience.

'Abd al-Nasir's Syrian interlocutors in this first series of talks were at an enormous personal disadvantage. Only one of them, Nihad Qasim, had met Nasir before, and he in any case was Nasir's man. Zuhur, the Ba'th representative, was a former school-teacher and editorial writer for *al-Ba'th* newspaper, who had lately risen to standing within the party. Although he had been a member of the 1954–8 Syrian parliament, he had had no previous experience as a minister or a negotiator. The other Syrians present were obscure army officers who during the union had stood in awe not only of 'Abd al-Nasir's Olympian figure but, for that matter, of Marshal 'Amir and the other Egyptian officials sitting beside Nasir. None of the Syrians were in a position to respond to Nasir's attack in comparable terms, or with comparable self-assurance. To them he was 'Mr President' or 'Your Excellency'; he called them by their first names.[5]

None the less the Syrians managed to voice their com-

---

[4] *Mahadir*, pp. 12–13.
[5] APD's erroneous replacement of first with last names has been corrected in passages cited.

plaints—the officers with diffidence, Zuhur with remarkable spirit. Every Egyptian officer in Syria during the
union, said General Qutayni, acted as if he were Gamal
'Abd al-Nasir, and Syrian officers felt themselves so
demoralized that by 28 September 1961 they felt no in-
centive to oppose the secession. Zuhur, for his part,
alleged that the Ba'th members had been systematically
slighted during the union and that the substitution of the
National Union organization for political parties had
created a 'vacuum' of political activity into which the
secessionists stepped.[6]

As for what the Party understands by freedom, socialism
and unity [he continued], the Party is proud that, after 15
years, these slogans have now become the whole Arab nation's
[thereby pointedly hinting that 'Abd al-Nasir himself had
borrowed his concepts from the Ba'th]. We have indeed read
the UAR Charter and we agree with most [*sic*] of what is in
it. But the Charter is not important. What is important is the
organization of the Arab Socialist Union, and we await the
results.

These were only preliminary remarks. Next day Zuhur
went much farther and considerably irritated 'Abd al-
Nasir. The real problem of the previous union, he alleged,
was that whereas the revolutionary movements in Syria
such as the Ba'th sprang from the people, in Egypt the
revolution had no original popular base and had consequently imposed its measures from above. Having eliminated Syrian parties, it proceeded along equally authori-
tarian lines in Syria.[7] Furthermore, Egypt, unlike Syria,
possessed an elaborately developed bureaucracy which
imposed itself on the Syrian army and civilian ministries
without any adaptation to local needs and attitudes. But
worse than this:

[6] Ibid. p. 14.   [7] Ibid. p. 23.

There was always the feeling that the Egyptian government was looking about for agents and was not anxious to deal with revolutionaries. . . . To rely solely on the secret service is very dangerous, for this service is merely [supposed to be] a force which aids popular organizations. As these organizations did not exist, the service became dominant. . . . Little confidence was placed in the Syrians. This may be due to the fact that the UAR authorities were dealing at first with bureaucrats and politicians. Top civil servants under non-revolutionary conditions are usually hypocritical, and politicians often attempt to advance themselves at each other's expense. . . .

This was too much for 'Abd al-Nasir. He denied that in all his twenty-one years of revolutionary activity he had ever relied on 'agents'. This was 'the kind of slander which was directed against the UAR from its earliest days with a view to destroying the Union. I would like you to name me one agent of ours in Syria. Name one.' (Sa'di promptly obliged by naming five.) Not only Nasir but also Nihad Qasim took offence, claiming that Zuhur had implied that he was one of Nasir's 'stooges', which Zuhur denied.[8] Already the Syrians were fighting among themselves.

Then 'Abd al-Nasir inquired who was ruling Syria. Well, said Qutayni, there was a Revolutionary Council of ten officers and ten civilians which would be responsible for legislation and policy planning. 'That won't do at all, Rashid', said Nasir, 'Give me the details.' Qutayni fumbled evasively. 'What I want to know is, who is on this Council with which we're supposed to contract a union. Am I to deal with ghosts?' asked Nasir, his temper

[8] Ibid. pp. 28–30. One of the Ba'thists who participated in this session has alleged to the author that a number of awkward details were edited out of this section of the transcript by the Egyptian publishers. One of these was an admission by 'Abd al-Nasir that Egypt did in fact resort to hiring supporters among editors of Lebanese newspapers and magazines, and had subsidized some seventeen of them. Another point, allegedly raised by Sa'di in informal conversation with Nasir after the session, concerned the Iraqi former Ba'th minister, Fu'ad al-Rikabi, whom the Iraqis charged with having pocketed £E20,000 intended as a subsidy to the party.

obviously rising. Again Qutayni mumbled incoherently, and again Nasir pressed for names. 'It is not possible to clarify some points', said Major Fahd al-Sha'ir. 'There is the Arab people of Syria, and the Arab Army of Syria.' 'Well', interjected 'Amir, 'doesn't anyone represent them?'

Finally, General Hariri intervened:

Actually, we have been trying to keep this secret, so as to maintain collective leadership, so that people will not gossip about what goes on in the meetings. But to begin with, of course, there is the Commander-in-Chief of the Army, the Minister of Defence, the Chief of Staff, the Deputy Chief of Staff, and various other ranks.

At length, under 'Abd al-Nasir's continued prodding, ten names were slowly produced. The civilian members had not been chosen yet, but one could get an idea of their likely composition by looking at the cabinet.

Here Qasim broke into the discussion to complain vehemently about Ba'thist domination in the cabinet and prospectively in the Council. It was absurd, he said, to pretend that other nationalist forces did not exist. 'We did not come here to discuss the composition of the Revolutionary Council or cabinet', objected Sha'ir. The argument raged on among the Syrians, until 'Abd al-Nasir intervened to repeat his own mistrust of the Ba'th and his fear of 'the hammer and the anvil'. 'But not one of the officers [on the Council] is Ba'thist', said Sha'ir disingenuously, himself a Ba'th supporter. 'They are all above partisanship.' Clearly Nasir did not believe him; he had already complained earlier on about the continued factionalism within the Syrian army. Out of 20 NRCC members, if 11 were Ba'thist they would control affairs, and that would be too much for him.[9]

Vainly the Ba'thists—Zuhur, Shabib, and Sa'di—protested their party's sincere intentions and attachment to

[9] *Mahadir*, pp. 43–51.

'Abd al-Nasir. Regardless of who was in the majority, insisted Shabib, the will of all parties to collaborate was what mattered. Even without any representation in the Syrian government at all, the Ba'th could obstruct the workings of a union between Egypt and Syria, and the Party Command in Damascus could incite the Iraqi Ba'th against Nasir as well. But such destructive ideas, and indeed all the evils of the Ba'th of which Nasir complained, according to Zuhur, had disappeared with the departure from the party of Akram Hawrani and his followers. As for Sa'di, he orated:

> My inspiration in political activity is based on morality. I would destroy my own name as a Ba'thist if it were in my nature to use the present state of affairs for a political manoeuvre to encircle or put pressure on the UAR between Syria and Iraq. . . . We had a high moral upbringing, and we did not go into politics in its classical sense [*sic*], to be corrupted. . . .[10]

As Sa'di went on bombastically Nasir's distaste for the Ba'th must have increased even more profoundly.

Little was being accomplished in these exchanges, except to keep the Ba'thists on the defensive. That in itself, however, was tactically important. 'Abd al-Nasir in the fourth session pursued this tactic with particular relentlessness at the expense of 'Abd al-Karim Zuhur. He began by accusing the Syrians of deceitfulness. Yesterday he had been told that the civilian members of the Syrian NRCC had not been chosen yet; but at a private meeting later on, Zuhur had indicated that they had been, and had given their names. Immediately Zuhur protested that he had been misunderstood, that nothing had been decided, and that he had only been speculating as to who the civilian members were likely to be. As 'Abd al-Nasir repeated the accusation, Zuhur became irritated: 'Mr President, I really do not think that one should pounce on [i.e. take

[10] Ibid. p. 55.

deliberate advantage of] another person's remarks.'
Furious at being talked back to with such effrontery,
Nasir scolded Zuhur like a schoolboy.

Nasir: 'Abd al-Karim, I never pounce on anyone's remarks.
Zuhur: I apologize, Mr President. I did not at all mean . . .
Nasir: We are here to remove all misunderstandings, and
to be perfectly frank with each other. To claim that I pounce
on your remarks is a shameful way of speaking which I simply
refuse to accept. I accepted all your remarks yesterday about
agents, etc. [but he had not!] because there was a principle at
stake. But I am not here to snipe at you. I heard what you
told me yesterday, I relayed it to my colleagues and we formed
our conclusions. Did you expect me not to tell my colleagues?
Zuhur: Of course not.
Nasir: Then tell me why I should snipe at you and distort
your remarks.
Zuhur: Mr President, I said this but I did not know . . .
Nasir: Had I not mentioned this matter now, I would not
have been perfectly sincere about unity. I welcome all self-
criticisms but your remark went beyond this limit.
Zuhur: Perhaps . . .
Nasir: Any amount of self-criticism is welcome and will not
annoy me in the least.

The browbeating continued for some time until 'Abd
al-Nasir finally accepted Zuhur's apologies. Nasir's view
of 'self-criticism' seems to have been somewhat one-sided
—indeed, later on he was to say much more provocative
things to Michel 'Aflaq and Salah al-Din Bitar than
Zuhur said to him—and one may wonder what kind of
atmosphere of 'understanding' Nasir hoped to establish.
It was, however, an effective way of reminding the Ba'thists
that they had come to Cairo as his petitioners. In the
midst of this lesson Shabib made a sensible observation
which pointed to the absurdity of Nasir's original complaint, but Nasir simply shrugged it off:

Shabib: But, Mr President, if he really wanted to intrigue, he would not have told you.

Zuhur: I even mentioned all our discussions to you.

Nasir: That is why it is better for me to say all this, rather than to mention behind your back that you came here to intrigue.

Finally, after this episode, 'Abd al-Nasir opened the question of the form of union that might be negotiated. But in reality it was another preliminary psychological manoeuvre, calculated to test his visitors' reactions and to remind them of the limits of their opportunities.

Nasir proposed that the union be formed in two stages: first Egypt and Syria for a trial period of four months, and then, if all went well, with Iraq as third partner. To placate those Syrians who considered Nasir a dictator, he was ready to step aside and support a union without Nasir. Alternatively, if the Syrians wanted Iraq included in the union to balance Egypt, let Syria and Iraq begin by uniting alone with Egypt and joining later.

It was easily predictable that both the Syrians and Iraqis should reject all these suggestions. A Syrian-Egyptian union without 'Abd al-Nasir was unthinkable, and various delegates hastened to pay him homage. 'President Nasir', declared Zuhur (anxious, perhaps, to be restored to favour), 'has no right to choose but is fated to lead the way, to receive all the shafts of the enemy, to be happy or unhappy depending on the state of the nation and to be harmed, too, depending on this state. He who heads a whole historical process must inevitably take up this stand.'

A union confined initially to Syria and Iraq was equally unthinkable. 'Throughout our history, we have always regarded Egypt as the focal point of Arab nationalism', declared Sha'ir with his accustomed poetic licence. Every-

F

one present, perhaps 'Abd al-Nasir most of all, was well aware that the weight of Nasir's prestige was the priceless asset that the Syrian and Iraqi delegations had come to Cairo to seek, and it was no doubt useful to Nasir to let them recall this fact for themselves.

An initial Syrian-Egyptian union, with 'Abd al-Nasir but without Iraq, was a more delicate matter, inasmuch as this was precisely what the Ba'th feared and what some of their opponents wanted. The Syrians, of course, refused it, on the grounds that public opinion would not accept the exclusion of Iraq. But they were in a difficult position. They needed Iraq, but they needed Nasir. What price must they pay in order to have both? Qasim pointedly remarked that 'if these doubts centre around the Ba'th, then their removal is possible. Our session today was for the purpose of discovering ways and means to remove these doubts, and we do not regard the Ba'th as the representative of Syria.'

'Abd al-Nasir himself minced no words in explaining his rationale, as if to remind the Ba'th of the cards he held. He prophesied with remarkable clarity what was in fact to happen:

When the Union of 1958 came into being, the Ba'th found that it could not agree with the UAR or any of the other unionist groups, i.e. with the so-called Nasirists. So the Ba'th withdrew from the government, and I consider this was a crime. In fact I said yesterday that the Ba'th undermined the Union. I am attempting to look ahead into the future. The Ba'th which is ruling Syria now will again not agree either with the UAR or the other unionist groups and Egypt will withdraw from this union at the end of four months. This is what I expect to happen and yet I agree to take the risk of another try, specifying, however, a four months' trial period. But before these four months are up, the Ba'th will start its manoeuvres, assuming that it will not have outgrown its bitterness. [It] will not withdraw but will attempt to make its position strong in Syria with the aid of certain military men. In this case, the UAR will withdraw from the union and that's that. Frankly, I should be anxious about Iraq in such an eventuality. I do not think that Iraq would be in a position to withstand the same setback that we withstood in 1961. . . .

I am certain that we shall not agree. Last time, the Ba'th withdrew in this criminal fashion. Well then, why is it that we run so eagerly after trouble, forming a union to be followed by a secession, then union and then another secession? Along with us, we should drag our people, who would eventually disavow the very idea of unity. Hence we have laid down a transitional period of four months during which we may reach an agreement, provided that we learn the lessons of the past and that we do not indulge in underhanded sniping and slander. If this union can live for four months I think it will be all right. But if the Syrian Ba'th is going to follow its old policy, then we shall clash.

It was left unsaid, though no doubt clearly understood, that by 'Abd al-Nasir's criteria, 'success' during these four months would mean confining the Ba'th to a limited role and placing ultimate power in other hands. The Iraqi Ba'th would then be faced with the prospect of entering into union between an Egyptian and a Syrian 'hammer and anvil'.

Syrian-Egyptian meetings

'Abd al-Nasir's wish that the crises and quarrels of the 1958 union be thrashed out with the Ba'th before a new union be negotiated, could not be adequately fulfilled by talking to 'Abd al-Karim Zuhur, who had been only a minor figure in the old days. For Nasir 'the Ba'th' meant Salah al-Din Bitar and Michel 'Aflaq themselves. Accordingly these two men, accompanied by the NRCC President Luay Atasi and the ever-present Fahd Sha'ir, came to Cairo for talks on 19 and 20 March.

In many ways the substance and atmosphere of this second round were a repetition of the previous one. As before, the primary purpose was not to negotiate but to 'clear the air', as 'Abd al-Nasir put it. Once again, only in greater detail, he enumerated his past grievances, browbeat his listeners, reiterated his lack of confidence in them as future partners, and contemptuously challenged their ideology. This time, however, he was talking to older men who should have been able to hold their own against him if anyone could, who had had many years' political experience as the leaders of a powerful international party and who—particularly 'Aflaq, revered by young Ba'thists as the party philosopher—enjoyed a considerable reputation as cultivated and articulate intellectuals. Furthermore, both of them had met the Egyptian President any number of times in 1958 and 1959 and could be presumed to have some sense of the most effective way to deal with him.

What is most remarkable about this second series of discussions is that if anything 'Abd al-Nasir dealt with 'Aflaq and Bitar more ruthlessly and effectively than he had with Zuhur. It was a remarkable display of the impact a powerful personality can have on negotiations: Nasir always supremely confident, always steering the discussion in the direction of his choice, always conscious of the substantive or psychological point at issue, blunt, forceful, clear and often witty in his expression, alternatively charming or bullying according to his purpose, not hesitating at times to harass, interrupt, or embarrass his visitors and decisively rejecting opposing claims or criticisms whenever he did not fancy their implications. By contrast, Bitar and 'Aflaq emerge from the record of the discussion as embarrassed, confused, tongue-tied, and generally ineffectual characters—a major consideration, no doubt, in the minds of the Egyptian authorities in publishing the talks later on.

In fairness it needs to be said that 'Aflaq and Bitar were

not the fools they seemed to be. Both of them were well known to be painfully slow and deliberate conversationalists, not given to the quick retorts at which 'Abd al-Nasir excels. Thus it was true that 'Aflaq had little to say, but this was partly because Nasir constantly interrupted him. Also, in the long discussions of ideology, as we shall see, it is likely that they were put off by Nasir's approach, which was to recite like a catechism an odd mixture of slogans from Egypt's National Charter, specific political and economic regulations, and Leninist dogmas. As for the discussion of events during the 1958 union, the Syrians were naturally reluctant to quarrel. It was they who had come to seek a new agreement and to win Nasir's acceptance; they meant little to him, but he meant everything to them. Underlining this consideration was the fact that the Ba'th, as an avowed champion of unity, had made it their official line to condemn the 1961 secession although they had been major victims of the union and although Bitar, much to his subsequent regret, had signed the infamous secession manifesto. Nasir did not let him forget this. He continually charged 'Aflaq and Bitar with having undermined the union, and it was true that they had done so. Given the nature of the union regime, the Ba'th's effort to protect its own interests was bound to undermine it, and a reasonable case could be made for doing so. But later, once they had accepted the line that secession was treason, the Ba'th leaders had forfeited the means of defending their own record. Bitar and 'Aflaq had come to Nasir with their hands tied behind their backs.

'Abd al-Nasir began by expatiating on the failure of the 1958 union. He admitted that it had been a mistake to disband all Syrian political parties. The difficulty was that the Syrian regime with which Egypt had united had included a variety of conflicting revolutionary and reactionary groups between whom it was impolitic to try to draw invidious distinctions. But a large part of the blame, he insisted, belonged to the Ba'th. The Ba'thists themselves had proposed that parties should be dissolved (they had of course done so only in anticipation that Nasir would demand it), then behaved as if they had been made an exception. He and Bitar had a 'long account' to settle. In December 1958 Bitar and other Ba'thists had resigned together from the government, in a conspiratorial manner, without warning and without having first detailed their complaints so that they might be dealt with. This had amounted to withdrawal from the union itself. Worse still, the Ba'thists had secretly attempted to persuade a number of Egyptian ministers to resign with them. After their resignations, the Ba'thists had spent the rest of the unity period making difficulties for the government, and when secession came, Bitar and Hawrani had signed a declaration in support of it.

Even while still in office, 'Abd al-Nasir charged, the Ba'th ministers had behaved badly. Bitar and Hawrani had constantly complained to him about each other behind each other's backs. In the fall of 1959, when 'Abd al-Hakim 'Amir had been sent to Syria, Bitar had told him the Ba'th could not work with Nasir but were prepared to co-operate with him.

Most disgracefully of all, 'Aflaq in 1958 had proposed that the UAR be directed by a secret six-men committee of whom the Syrian members would be Hawrani, Bitar, and himself. And yet now everything was being blamed on Hawrani. (The proposal had only been 'Aflaq's idea, Bitar interjected.)

'Aflaq and Bitar, despite the handicaps under which they laboured, did make some effort to fight back. They had voluntarily disbanded themselves in the expectation that they would be given a real opportunity to take a lead in building the new organization, the National Union, and that their participation in the government would carry more than nominal responsibility. They had waited as long as they did to resign only in order to spare 'Abd al-Nasir further problems in the light of the 1958 Iraqi revolution, for in practice they felt that Nasir's neglect of them had all but constituted dismissal since mid-1958. When they decided to resign, explained 'Aflaq, they considered it best to try to persuade Egyptian ministers to join them so that their resignation would not carry the implication of a Syrian-Egyptian dispute and thus endanger the union itself. It was understandable that Nasir had acquired a bad impression of the party from Hawrani and his associates; but could he not have seen that the party comprised two wings, of which Hawrani's was destined in time to go its own way? (Nasir: 'What do you take me for, a prophet? . . . We were under the impression that Hawrani was the leader of the party.') In any case, the Ba'th ministers felt they had no choice but to resign, in protest against the government's policies. Then, 'Aflaq asserted, 'from our resignation till the secession, a period of nine months, we were subjected to a barrage of slander, insults and persecution' by the regime's publicity media.

It was when the conversation moved to questions of ideology and programmes that the Syrians appeared in the least favourable light. What, 'Abd al-Nasir wanted to know, had the Ba'th to say about party organization, freedom, democracy, and socialism? He answered this question himself: the Ba'th failed to explain its concepts, because it did not really have any. It was too wrapped up in vague theorizing to think systematically or practically.

For the past fifteen years, the Ba'th Party has never fully clarified its concept of freedom. I have read all their writings and have looked in vain for a clear definition of freedom. . . . Neither in ['Aflaq's] books nor in any others have I been able to find a proper definition. Then again, their concept of social-ism is vague. . . . I once asked Akram Hawrani for the socialist programme of the Party and he said that they only had slogans, not a programme.

By contrast, Nasir reminded his listeners time and again, the UAR had complete answers to all these questions, fully explained in the National Charter.

As we understand it and as it is found in the Charter, freedom means a free country and a free citizen. The Charter explains this in great detail and perfectly clearly. Socialism, again, implies sufficiency and justice and the Charter also defines these two terms very fully. Unity is a popular, historical, and actual will, and the Charter devotes a whole chapter to con-stitutional unity in all its forms. The socialist path is defined, beginning with internal trade and ending with popular con-trol over the means of production, passing through agricul-ture, the private sector, and the public sector. All national activity is fully defined in the Charter.

. . . What is implied . . . by the freedom of the individual? We maintained that this freedom entails total freedom for the people and its denial to enemies of the people. . . . We also advocated that democracy, socialism, and freedom are inter-dependent. Now then, how does the Ba'th define democracy?

Bitar and 'Aflaq might be forgiven for finding difficulty in responding in comparable terms to this catalogue of 'complete definitions'. It would have stood them in good stead to point out that democracy, socialism, etc. are not easily summed up in a such superficial slogans; but 'Abd al-Nasir's recitation seemed to paralyse them, and perhaps they hesitated to appear critical of the Charter, in which Nasir took such pride. But Nasir in any case had come to give lessons, not to receive them.

'Aflaq: . . . I believe that you do not lack a definition of demo-cracy and socialism but I have observed that, sometimes, socialism has taken the place of democracy.

Nasir: Have you read the Charter?

'*Aflaq:* Yes.

Nasir: Then it appears that you were reading one line and skipping the next. It is not at all what you imagine. Our revolution was the first to call for social democracy, meaning that political [democracy] was inconceivable without social democracy. This fact led us to socialism and to the inevitability of socialism as a prerequisite for true democracy. Otherwise, democracy would have become the dictatorship of capitalism and feudalism. This is what is generally termed bourgeois democracy. But there was never any mention [*sic*] of socialism taking the place of democracy. . . .

The Ba'th, 'Abd al-Nasir maintained, only displayed their naïveté in charging the Egyptian leaders with dictatorship. 'You imagine that we simply give orders and the country is run accordingly. You are greatly mistaken.' They were equally naïve to suppose that a revolutionary government could wait for the public to present its demands. As a revolutionary, he explained, one had to take the lead and not sit back expecting popular demands to crystallize spontaneously. The Soviets did not wait after 1917. The 'vanguard' must formulate its objectives and then act on its own initiative. The meaning of leadership— here Nasir was quoting, consciously or not, from Lenin— was to grasp the needs of society and then act upon them. Accepting persons of unknown orientation to share in leadership would destroy this purpose. The Egyptian leadership anticipated the masses' needs before the latter were themselves aware of them. The leadership was the vanguard, because it worked in the masses' interest.[11]

Thus 'Abd al-Nasir defended his record against Ba'th innuendoes. The Ba'th set themselves up as defenders of democracy; yet on their own admission their party only had about 10,000 members, whereas the Arab Socialist Union had 5 million.

[11] *Mahadir*, pp. 154–5.

Do you fancy that government by the people, even though you have elections, is merely a few people sitting in a room and deciding affairs? You are mistaken, for then you would have isolated the whole people and ruled as a tiny minority.

Even in Russia, in 1917 ['Abd al-Nasir added in a later session], Lenin did not rely on the party alone but used the Soviets. . . . In his first five-year plan, all authority was transferred to the Soviets by Lenin. . . . Party dictatorship can never succeed. However, if you have a dictatorship of the working people, which is in effect a democracy, you will gain adherents the whole time.

All these ideological discussions, of course, reflected differences of practical purpose between 'Abd al-Nasir and the Ba'th, in particular the Ba'th's determination to establish for itself as a party a prominent role in the future union, and Nasir's desire to submerge them in a wider front. Consequently it was unfortunate for the Ba'th that Bitar and 'Aflaq found so little to say in response to Nasir's ideological exposés and challenges. Not only did they allow themselves to seem bereft of all but the vaguest ideas ('The proper solution [for the problems of Arab unity] lies in society: education and love', said 'Aflaq), but they ended by at least appearing to accept the principle of sharing power inside Syria.

In other matters as well the Syrians fell in weakly with 'Abd al-Nasir's views. Thus when Atasi proposed the immediate renationalization of Syrian banks,[12] the following conversation ensued:

Bitar: There is first the stage of 'Arabization' of banks.
Atasi: You mean nationalization.
Bitar: No, I mean 'Arabization' first. . . . There are two stages, first 'Arabization' and then nationalization.
Nasir: This is what we did in Syria during the Union.
Bitar: Yes, indeed. These decrees are well known.
Atasi: We know them, as they all came at a certain period.

[12] The Syrian government nationalized the banks on 2 May.

Nasir: I do not see the need for two stages.
Bitar: I agree.

But even when the Syrians gave signs of willingness to accommodate Nasir on the question of unified leadership, it did not appear that agreement was really what he wanted. Atasi at one point proposed that the 'political bureau' ruling the union should include one member from each of the three countries, plus the President (i.e. 'Abd al-Nasir) as chairman. 'Thus, with the President, there would be four members of the Council and the problem of being caught between the hammer and the anvil, as your Excellency puts it, would not arise.' Nasir received this suggestion with what seems like deliberate obtuseness:

Nasir: Fine, let us assume there are two representatives . . .
Atasi: Why two?
Nasir: Suppose every region has two representatives and I am out of this council, who then would be chairman, and how should we proceed?
Atasi: I am saying one representative, Your Excellency.
Nasir: Let us suppose there were two . . . [Then, changing his tack] Let us suppose there are three members, plus a fourth, on the basis of a balance, or two from the Ba'th. Then two-thirds would be Ba'th, one-third Socialist Union. This means Ba'th preponderance which would cause it to falter in its steps.
Atasi: Another solution, to be practical, which I am trying to be, would be to have two members of the Socialist Union, one Syrian [Ba'thist], and one Iraqi Ba'thist, with Your Excellency as chairman. I believe that mutual trust exists. The President would inevitably be above all parties.
Sha'ir: (Breaking in suddenly after long silence): Why don't we have a Union Council, as in the USSR?
'Aflaq: Of course.
Sha'ir: I think we might have a Higher Union Council . . .[13]

[13] Throughout the talks Sha'ir, in his frequent interventions, seemed to typify the mentality of young officers who have entered the arena of high

Nasir: But this would change nothing. The basic problem remains, namely, of whom shall this council be composed? If it happens that you have an Iraqi Ba'thist, a Syrian Ba'thist and an Egyptian, then the Ba'th would actually be running the state.

The second series of talks broke up on this confused note, with 'Aflaq, Bitar, and their colleagues trying to learn precisely what 'Abd al-Nasir required of them and Nasir continuing to harp on the seemingly insoluble problem of establishing confidence, and implying that it would somehow be up to the Ba'th to do something to facilitate this. 'It seems to me', remarked 'Aflaq rather pathetically at the last meeting, 'that the problem is: are there any basic disagreements between us?' Hours of talk had failed to answer this question. By avoiding a prompt and clear statement of his own terms and reiterating his themes of mistrust, Nasir presumably intended to put the Ba'th under as heavy as possible a psychological obligation to try to mollify him. His essential requirement was that the Ba'th should not only share power with him on the federal level, but with his partisans within Syria and Iraq. When 'Aflaq assured him that 'the Ba'th would never interfere in the affairs of Egypt', Nasir seized on this statement and berated 'Aflaq: 'You don't interfere in Egypt and we don't interfere in Syria. What kind of proposal is that? . . . Are you proposing that we divide the union up? It would be far better for us to stay as we are.' Furthermore, as he observed on a later occasion, if the federal government were directed by a Coalition Front of party representatives from each country, rather than a fully integrated organization, then 'each member of the Front will say that he must

---

politics via one coup or another with no qualification save a vague and aimless ideological enthusiasm. At one moment he proposed 'a one-party system like that of the Soviet Union'; a few minutes later he was calling for 'a two-party system like that of Britain' (*Mahadir*, pp. 171 and 175).

return to his region to get endorsement for his views. The result would be silence, followed by coffee-drinking.' In order to remind 'Aflaq and Bitar of the weakness of their bargaining position, he suggested that his Arab Socialist Union be permitted to operate in Syria and Iraq, in competition with the Ba'th, and that the Ba'th be allowed to organize in Egypt. The Ba'th leaders, of course, rejected this plan with alacrity. 'But you have vast means', complained 'Aflaq. 'You say that you have neither the will nor the means', retorted Nasir, 'and I say we do not have the will but possess the means.' He did indeed have the means, and the Ba'th had reason to fear that if they did not make the necessary concessions, he might develop the will too.

The last round of talks

The Syrians then went home. 'Aflaq, said to have been very angry over the treatment he had received from 'Abd al-Nasir, remained there. After a fortnight Bitar and Atasi, accompanied by an enlarged delegation, returned to Cairo for the definitive round of negotiations with both the Egyptians and Iraqis.

Once again, however, 'Abd al-Nasir said he was not yet ready to get down to business. Since the last meetings new developments had revived his mistrust of the Ba'th, in the form of 'underhand sniping' in editorials in *al-Ba'th* newspaper, as a result of which he had allowed Hasanayn Haykal to retaliate in *al-Ahram*. Summoning the Syrians to a separate meeting, Nasir demanded an explanation.

The editorials of which 'Abd al-Nasir complained were actually rather mild pieces. One of them, which Haykal particularly singled out for attack, entitled 'More Royalist than the King', seemed not at all to be directed against Nasir or Egypt but only against Syrians who, in Nasir's name, demanded the immediate revival of the 1958 union without Iraq, at a time when Nasir himself had agreed to the principle of a tripartite union. It reminded these people that the Ba'th had rejected an appeal by Akram Hawrani for a bilateral Syrian-Iraqi union, for 'we have not lost even for one moment our conviction that Egypt must be at the head and heart of any union'. It called on them 'not to sink in the mire of a "neo-secessionism" comparable to the opportunistic secessionism of the apostate Hawrani'. The closest the editorial came to criticism of the Egyptian regime was to say that the 1958 union 'was only a step along the road, and not an idol for us to bow down to and march around'.[14]

Somewhat sharper had been *al-Ba'th*'s editorial of 27 March, which declared that 'the process of building unity . . . is not merely one of obtaining the people's consent in a referendum', and that in the previous union 'the masses were kept in storage' so that the forces of secession 'found the arena completely empty'. Only an effective popular organization could fill this vacuum, but such an organization was not to be built simply by 'heaping together workers, peasants, and progressive intellectuals'— an implied reference, of course, to Egypt's Arab Socialist Union.

Seizing upon the title 'More Royalist than the King' and blatantly distorting its meaning, Haykal had retorted: 'Who is the king referred to here? Is it Gamal 'Abd al-Nasir? . . . Gamal 'Abd al-Nasir is not demanding Syria's throne, nor is he dreaming of finding himself again at the balcony of the guest palace in Damascus receiving the greetings of his subjects.'[15]

Now Nasir confronted Bitar, charging that 'the Ba'th is attempting treacherously to undermine our coming together'. Bitar replied by complaining about Haykal's

[14] *al-Ba'th*, 23 Mar. 1963.   [15] *al-Ahram*, 31 Mar. 1963.

interpretation of the articles and insisting that in reality there were serious ideological differences between Nasir and the Ba'th which it was legitimate for the press to discuss. Seeming to forget the round of talks that had only recently ended, he said: 'We have never really sat down to a long session in which these differences could be brought up and ideas exchanged'. In any case, added Bitar the next day, he had not seen the articles in *al-Ba'th*. This gave 'Abd al-Nasir the chance to make a fool of him:

Nasir: Don't you read the Lebanese press? It was also published in Lebanon [as well as in the Paris *Figaro*].

Bitar: We have not seen it so as to refute it.

Nasir: Don't you read the Lebanese press?

Bitar: No, we don't.

Nasir: Neither the French nor the Lebanese press?

Bitar: No, we don't. They do not enter Syria so . . .

Nasir: But this is incredible! What kind of talk is that?

Bitar: Your Excellency, when you read them, please contact us.

Nasir: You don't read the Syrian, Lebanese, or French press?! How on earth do you govern your country?

Bitar: Well, then, let someone get in touch with us and inform us. We don't have the time to read.

Nasir: Before I go to sleep, for example, I read all the Lebanese, French, British, and Syrian press. . . .

For Bitar to insist that 'serious ideological differences' underlay the problem was a first-class tactical error which 'Abd al-Nasir was glad to seize upon. It offered him a pretext to string the discussions out even further than he had done on an even less promising basis, keeping the Syrian delegation tied up in Cairo while their month-old regime tottered in Damascus. Alternatively, should the Syrians break off the talks on an obscure doctrinal issue, they would have to bear the discredit.

Pressed by 'Abd al-Nasir to explain these 'differences',

the Ba'thists quickly retreated. They promised to explain them once the Iraqis were present. But that evening when the three delegations convened, Talib Shabib, the Iraqi Foreign Minister and much the most articulate of all the Ba'thists, declared: 'It would be very difficult to say that there are ideological differences. . . . As a member of the Iraqi delegation and as a Ba'thist, I affirm that there are no differences in ideology.'

But, said Nasir, Bitar and Zuhur had insisted that there were such differences. 'We arranged this meeting precisely in order to discuss them'. 'The question has to do with defining the scope of theory', explained Zuhur lamely.

Hence if we include the method of implementation in the meaning of 'theory', we can say that there are ideological differences. Otherwise . . . we cannot. . . . Taking what Talib [Shabib] has said into consideration, we seem to be agreed that there are no basic differences and, by implication, no ideological differences.

Bitar, who only the day before had said he could expound the ideological differences 'for months', now retracted. 'I do not believe there are ideological differences. As others have mentioned, in reality the various revolutionary movements all have the same aim. . . .'[16]

It was all very embarrassing. Were there ideological disagreements or not? No one was sure. The dismal discussion of the meaning of democracy, liberty, etc. began all over again. Colonel Muhammad 'Umran of the Syrian NRCC presented a simple soldier's view:

I believe the content of freedom and democracy is clear, namely, that the people must exercise full authority. But at what point can they in fact do so? Here is a point at issue. But in reality, the conception of freedom and democracy is clear:

[16] The last two sentences are altered from a misleading translation in *APD*; cf. *Mahadir*, p. 295.

a people exercising its authority. When, however, is another question. . . .

Since the first round of talks 'Abd al-Nasir had been trying in vain to elicit a firm statement of principle from the Ba'th as to whether they favoured the continuance of multi-party activity. Having long posed as champions of democratic procedures in Syria, and complained after 1958 of Nasir's dissolution of parties, they were now faced with the demand of pro-Nasir parties that they share the power they had at last acquired for themselves in Damascus. Nasir now drew from Shibli al-'Aysami, Syrian Minister of Agrarian Reform, the admission that the party's earlier conception of democracy had 'evolved'. The Ba'th was now 'tending to view freedom as properly belonging to the working classes and to other socialist-minded bodies. It may, therefore, be finally forced to adopt a single-party system as its policy.' 'I conclude, Your Excellency', observed Luay al-Atasi sagely, 'that a detailed or specific definition of freedom is now difficult to arrive at.' Indeed it was. The ideological explorations drifted to an end on this perplexed note. Nasir next day delivered a sound verdict: 'In yesterday's discussions we went round in circles, creating all sorts of social, political, and military vacuums.'

Negotiating for union

At last it was time to bargain.

The delegations now took up in earnest the question of forming a unified political leadership, and found themselves altogether unable to agree. 'Abd al-Nasir's view, which he had repeated since the beginning of the talks, was that while he was willing to accept even the loosest confederation, if a real union of the three countries was desired then it would be essential to settle the leadership

G

problem in advance by merging the organizational struc-
tures of the various parties into a single body. Otherwise
party leaders, retaining separate party loyalties, would for
ever quarrel and confidence would never be solidly
established.

Both the Syrian and Iraqi Ba'thists, on the other hand,
favoured putting this problem off. Let the unified Arab
state be established and begin its work, under the guidance
of a simple coalition of the leaders of the three countries,
they said. In time a fully united political leadership could
be expected to evolve naturally; for the Ba'th did not consider 'Abd al-Nasir's Arab Socialist Union its rival but its
partner, and they were agreed on ideological fundamentals.

But 'how can one create a state without first agreeing
about its political organization?' asked 'Abd al-Nasir. The
Ba'thists were in the absurd position of arguing on the one
hand that finding a formula now for merging party leader-
ships was too difficult, and on the other hand that finding
one later would be easy. Then why was it so difficult to
agree now? There was no direct answer. Instead the
Ba'thists urged that they should proceed with negotiation
of the constitutional framework of the future union. Once
they had settled the distribution of powers within the
federal government, and between it and the three provincial governments, it would be easier to deal with the
leadership question.

At length 'Abd al-Nasir fell in with this proposal. The
Syrians had already drafted an outline of their own proposals, and a committee was now formed under the chair-
manship of the Egyptian Vice-President Kamal al-Din
Husayn. But when the committee presented its draft the
discussions became snarled over the question of the allot-
ment of powers to each of the two proposed houses of
parliament, the presidency, and the still undefined council
of joint political leadership. The Ba'thists wished to invest

predominant power within the Federal Assembly, or upper house, in which each of the three countries would be equally represented, and either to set up a select committee for 'political leadership' within this chamber, empowered to supervise the branches of government as a whole, or alternatively to embody this leadership in a Presidential Council surrounding the head of state. Either arrangement seemed well calculated to restrict Egyptian power. Correspondingly Nasir sought to emphasize the powers of the National Assembly, or lower house, with representation proportional to population and thus a three-to-one Egyptian majority, and to avoid the creation of a Presidential Council. Given the existence of two Houses of Parliament, a cabinet, a Prime Minister, and a President, he argued, the President's powers would already be small, except for a veto power similar to that of the American President; and the members of a Presidential Council would find nothing to do. They would, however, deprive the President of his control of the veto, since he would need the concurrence of a majority of them to be able to use it. 'Our real problem which is turning up all the time', Nasir commented, 'is the absence of unified political action. . . . Wherever we go, this problem stares us in the face and impedes our progress.'

Forgetting that only shortly before they had insisted on putting this question off, the Ba'thists now suddenly agreed on its urgency. For if they were to offset the Egyptians' constitutional influence, with 'Abd al-Nasir insisting on the powers of the lower house, perhaps the only way would be to circumvent these powers through some kind of joint leadership council after all. But there seemed to be no convenient and mutually acceptable means of fitting this body into a formal framework. Nasir, accused so often in the past of dictatorship, was now demanding effective popular representation and accepting a relatively weak presidency. When Zuhur proposed that parliamentary powers be exercised by a tripartite political bureau modelled on the Presidium of the Supreme Soviet, Nasir retorted: 'It is a tempting solution to our difficulties but then we would be charged not only with dictatorship but with a rootless tyranny.'

Finally, the Syrians and Iraqis accepted a draft along 'Abd al-Nasir's lines. According to the final agreement signed on 17 April, the President would appoint a Prime Minister and cabinet responsible to the lower (Egyptian-dominated) house; there would be no Presidential Council, and the three Vice-Presidents, one from each region, would only hold such powers as the President might choose to delegate to them. The President was empowered to veto legislative acts and could be overridden only by a three-fourths vote of both houses. He would make all major appointments and would be Commander-in-Chief of the armed forces. In a last-minute compromise Nasir also secured the right of the President to dissolve the Parliament.

The agreement also specified the creation of 'political fronts' in each country combining 'all unionist, socialist, and democratic forces', and 'a unified political leadership' at the federal level, but without incorporating these bodies into the constitutional structure, and consequently without any particular assurance that they would hold decisive influence. Both the local fronts and the political leadership at the federal level would be bound by majority decisions, with the fronts bound by the federal leadership's decisions. 'This leadership', declared the agreement, 'shall gradually establish a unified political organization that will lead national political action inside and outside the Federation, and will work to mobilize popular forces. . . . But this does not mean the dissolution of existing unionist parties.'[17]

[17] For the full text of the agreement see *APD*, pp. 227–46.

What did this mean? Surely the continuance of existing parties was inconsistent with a 'unified political organization'. Later the Ba'th leaders explained this contradiction by saying that the issue of parties had not been agreed upon, and it was left for a final round of discussion (along with other undecided points) before the formal ceremony at which the agreement would be signed. But when they entered the conference room, they alleged, they found the press and photographers present and on the table before them, ready for signature, a document worded according to Egyptian wishes, providing *inter alia* for the eventual creation of a 'unified political organization'. They hastily and surreptitiously managed to add a line in their own handwriting stating that 'this does not mean the dissolution of existing political parties', which they angrily persuaded 'Abd al-Nasir to accept after the ceremony. Other points were left as the Egyptians wanted them.

Regardless of the truth or falsity of this story, it is clear that there was no real agreement on the prospective character and function of the 'unified political leadership' or of the fronts in the three countries. Nor was there agreement on the structure of the provisional body, the Presidential Council, that would rule the union during the transitional period; for both the Ba'th and their opponents were constantly making mental calculations of the balance of votes that each proposed formula would create. On this issue the Ba'th eventually had their way: the membership of the Council would be on the basis of equality between the three countries, without regard to population. It was consequently in their interest to secure as long a transition period as possible, especially as in any case they were still faced with much political and administrative confusion in their countries.

In the penultimate meeting before signature of the agreement, on 13 April, the Ba'thists announced their

demands. Shabib wanted a long preliminary period—six
months rather than the proposed two—before the formal
declaration of unity. Then he and Zuhur both insisted on
a further transition period of at least two years before the
projected constitution should take effect. Zuhur explained:

> We cannot hold elections now, for we should have to rig
> them in order to avoid Ma'mun Kuzbari getting into power.
> We must have a long period of a strong regime which can
> achieve something before holding elections. . . . A Revolution
> cannot be democratic in character, Your Excellency. The
> government must direct from above and must penetrate down
> to the classes which it wishes to draw out into public life.

There had been earlier occasions when 'Abd al-Nasir himself had invoked similar considerations. He had once
warned the Syrians, for instance, that reactionaries could
be prevented from dominating the political and social life
of the country from behind the scenes only by the applica-
tion of socialist measures.

> When a revolution assumes power it must know how to
> keep it and has therefore to deprive its enemies of their essen-
> tial weapons. . . . Reaction is, to begin with, stronger than the
> Revolution, especially if this latter's aims are vague. . . . The
> people for whose sake you carry through your socialist measures
> are very difficult to assemble, but reactionaries can be col-
> lected together at a minute's notice at 'Al-Sharq' Club in
> Damascus. . . .[18]

But this time Nasir's attention was not focused on ideological instruction but on a negotiating point. He had won
his way on the distribution of constitutional powers and
did not wish to see it slip away. Without the constitution
and the National Assembly, and without any firmly
agreed plan for sharing leadership in Syria and Iraq, he
would simply have to begin the union in partnership with

[18] See also *Mahadir*, p. 163.

whatever regimes existed in Damascus and Baghdad; and these were presently dominated by the Ba'th. Any tripartite directorate or Presidential Council for the transition period, without an Assembly to fall back upon, would put him in the very position he sought to avoid.

He was at least able to make the Ba'thists uncomfortable.

Why do you suppose I have consented that the President of the Republic should have little or no authority? [he demanded]. It is because of your talk of tyranny and dictatorship. . . . This constitution is based on the draft presented by the Syrian delegation. We felt, after all that has been written about dictatorship, that you wanted a parliamentary democracy—and so we agreed. . . . We have argued all along on the assumption that our government would be parliamentarian. Now you do not want a parliament. Has our discussion all been in vain?

Zuhur and Shabib argued that they only wished to postpone, not cancel, the implementation of the constitution. They needed more time in their countries to begin their revolutionary programmes before rushing into parliamentary elections. If it occurred to 'Abd al-Nasir to ask why they were seeking unity at all while confronted with such urgent domestic challenges, he did not do so; but no doubt he was well aware of the answer: they wanted the prestige of his name, but without his interference, to bolster their authority.

I believe that our union is hopelessly feeble [he said]. The only strong link binding it together is the National Assembly. . . . If this National Assembly does not exist, then our union will in reality be a secession in the garb of a union. . . . We imagined that [a] transitional period of one year would suffice for the creation of a federal administration. This is why we agreed to all your comments, additions, and subtractions [actually he had not done so], because we imagined that the National Assembly would be holding the union together.

'If we implemented this constitution straight away', replied Zuhur, echoing 'Abd al-Nasir's previously expressed views, 'we should have to renounce our two revolutions and make way for reactionaries and secessionists who could then simply do away with the federation.'

I cannot for the life of me see why we were discussing this constitution then [Nasir retorted]. Why could we not simply have postponed this discussion until the end of this transitional period? And then, who knows what will happen three or four years from now? . . . Meanwhile, who is to rule the Republic?

A revolutionary body, as in all revolutions [said Zuhur].

Where is this body? [asked Nasir]. They will be at each other's throats in no time.

Nasir had scored an impressive debating point, but he did not have his way. The next morning he met the Iraqis privately and acceded to their plea for more time. He agreed to a five-months' delay before the union would be proclaimed, and a further transition period of twenty months before the constitution would take effect.

It was now the turn of the Nasirist members of the Syrian delegation, Nihad al-Qasim and Hani al-Hindi, to be dismayed. 'I must say that our conclusions are somewhat surprising', protested Hindi. 'If each region is to tackle its own problems independently [until the end of the transition period], our worries will increase, and you know exactly what these problems are.' Thus Hindi implied that the Ba'th in Damascus could be expected to use the opportunity to relegate him and his friends to limbo. His fears were fully justified, though it took not two years but only two weeks for them to be confirmed.

Thus the negotiations ended with an agreement to postpone the implementation of full union for over two years, and with only a vague outline of commitments for the interim period. During that period it could be expected that at best each country would be largely responsible for its own affairs while acting in close consultation with its partners, while at worst, collaboration would break down at an early stage, the entire scheme of union would collapse, and Ba'thists and Nasirists would resort to an open trial of strength.

Agreement to agree

The main theme throughout the talks had been the reciprocal attitude of mistrust between the Ba'th and 'Abd al-Nasir and his friends. Nasir kept bringing it up; the Ba'th kept playing it down; but both sides shared it equally. The Ba'th were not eager to share power in Syria or Iraq, and given Nasir's openly announced position, they were bound in any case to look to their own defences. Almost the whole of the talks appeared to be a game of cat-and-mouse, of psychological and diplomatic manoeuvring in which no satisfactory outcome was really possible. For it was clear that the Ba'th detested their rivals, particularly the Arab Nationalist Movement—a feeling which was fully reciprocated—and regarded them as opportunistic exploiters of 'Abd al-Nasir's name ('more royalist than the king') or even as his actual stooges, while Nasir's chief purpose was to force them to move aside and make equal room for the ANM and the others. From the very beginning Nasir had imposed an unacceptable condition, by vowing that he would unite with Syria but not with the Ba'th. The Ba'th, perhaps, should have returned home on the spot; instead they stayed and paid lip-service to his terms, declaring their readiness to co-operate and eventually even to merge with the Nasirists. But they never gave serious evidence of being reconciled to this, and never seemed to abandon hope that in practice 'Abd al-Nasir would tacitly give them the free hand they wanted.

Consequently the search for a formula for the unification of political leadership was fruitless. Ultimately it boiled down to the question of confidence, which was lacking. The agreement was no more than a statement of good intentions for the future, it being left to each country to take certain decisions and steps on its own initiative. Each must create its own Front, its own legislature, its own charter of political principles, and its own representation on certain joint committees and on the transitional Presidential Council; and then each must organize its own plebiscite. Given the state of affairs in both Syria and Iraq, it was unlikely that these steps could be completed satisfactorily. While 'Abd al-Nasir directed all his attack against the Syrian branch of the Ba'th, this was only for tactical reasons: if anything, the prospects for effective representation of his partisans in Iraq were even worse. (At one point in the talks Hani Hindi had tried to raise the question of the Arab Nationalist Movement's position in Iraq, only to receive an utter rebuff from Sa'di and Shabib and only perfunctory support from Nasir.)[19] Nasir's tactic was presumably dictated by the calculation that he was presently on much stronger ground in Syria, and that after securing his terms there, he could then bring overwhelming pressure on the Iraqis.

Conversely, the major object of the Syrian Ba'th was to gain some kind of explicit or implicit acknowledgement from Nasir of their legitimacy. They were consequently reluctant to retort to his insults, and restricted themselves to making their excuses and proclaiming their goodwill; for they could not afford to be the ones to break off the talks. Their denial of any intention to wield a 'hammer and anvil' against him may have been genuine enough: their primary interest was defensive, to be confirmed in their current position of power and perhaps also to obtain a

[19] *APD*, pp. 176–7.

major voice in the future pan-Arab policies of the projected Union, for example, *vis-à-vis* Jordan, Yemen, and Saudi Arabia. This position was suggested in 'Aflaq's ill-fated assurance that 'the Ba'th would never interfere in the internal affairs of Egypt', and in 'Abd al-Nasir's success in calling the Ba'th's bluff by offering the prospect of free party competition in all countries, including Egypt. The Ba'th could only be embarrassed by this, for they had no hopes in Egypt yet grievously feared Nasirite competition in Syria.

'You are asking something for nothing', 'Abd al-Nasir in effect told the Ba'th. 'If you want my endorsement you will have to settle for a reduced position in Syria and make room for my supporters.' Were he to let the Ba'th have its own way, Nasir would be declaring his own impotence in Arab affairs outside Egypt, and would lose the initiative altogether; for the Ba'th, whatever else it might be, was known to be a party outside his control. Nasirists elsewhere, in Jordan for example, would draw the lesson of his impotence, while in Egypt itself it would be seen that his pan-Arab policy consisted of writing blank cheques to other people's movements. He was on solid ground in declaring, as he did more than once in the talks, that a division of spheres of control between himself and the Ba'th would be no better than the Arab League. At least for Egypt this was so; for the Ba'th it might be the prelude to the growth of their influence elsewhere.

The Syrians and 'Abd al-Nasir both seemed always acutely conscious of the parallel between 1958 and 1963. They alluded to this symbolically when Bitar and 'Aflaq arrived 19 March: Nasir remarked that in 1958 he had said he thought five years' time was needed before union could be properly established, and Bitar rejoined that five years had now passed.[20] Each side's observations on

[20] *Mahadir*, p. 93.

the experience of the previous union bore their current implications. Thus Nasir's principal complaints—that the Ba'th ministers had resigned collectively, that 'Aflaq had sought the creation of a secret Ba'th-Egyptian steering committee—reflected on the Ba'th's quest for a privileged position. Similarly the Ba'thists' criticism of the disbanding of parties in 1958 and the alleged 'vacuum' that resulted under the National Union organization seemed a way of saying, 'now you must realize that you need us in order to fill that vacuum'. Their allegations of Egyptian dependence on 'agents' likewise could be taken as a veiled reference to present-day Syrian Nasirists, and Nihad al-Qasim was quite right to object to this implication. The discussion of the former union was thus a *sotto-voce* exchange of present bargaining positions. (The unhappy and absent figure of Akram Hawrani served as a safety-valve in this game: when the accusations seemed too grave, the Ba'thists—and occasionally Nasir—put the blame on him.)

ʳ 'Abd al-Nasir conducted the negotiations with great skill. His personality dominated the sessions, and he took full advantage. He could feel free to heap the harshest criticisms on 'Aflaq and Bitar, to bully them, to make jokes at their expense; they could hardly respond in kind. Consistently he strove to ensure that the psychological burden in the negotiations rested on their shoulders. They were his clients, and he addressed them as such. Any criticism or innuendo from them that touched his prestige he flung back at them, making their complaints a cause for complaints of his own. He gave 'Aflaq a particularly miserable time, dismissing his twenty years of intellectual endeavour as a university don might reject a dull student's research essay. In fact, the entire record of the talks, and especially the ideological discussions, call to mind a rather didactic professor conducting a seminar. Nasir used the conversations on ideology to embarrass the Ba'th and destroy their self-assurance. In 1958 they had seemed to think that he needed their sophistication: now, he told them, even in their own chosen field he had no need of them; in fact he had plenty to teach them. Some of his ideological discourses, especially those concerning parties and social classes, bore a more practical purpose as well: to show the Ba'th that their organization was too exclusive and too lacking in grass roots support to rule effectively.

The negotiations had not been a solid diplomatic success for 'Abd al-Nasir, however, for he had won no vital commitments except moral ones. What he had accomplished was to play the part that his reputation as the champion of pan-Arabism demanded, while protecting his interests against the risk of serious damage. The all-important commitment he had secured for the preliminary period, which would have to be tested immediately, was for the formation of acceptable coalitions in Syria and Iraq. If, miraculously, this came to pass, then Nasir would be protected against a Ba'thist 'hammer and anvil' and would gain leadership of a powerful union. If it did not, he would have ample time to withdraw with his prestige intact, charging the Ba'th with bad faith and publishing the record of the negotiations to substantiate the charge. His regime could easily do without unity, or even amity; for the Ba'th governments this would be more difficult.

4

Collapse

There is no one in Syria more Nasirist than the Ba'thists.

SAMI AL-JUNDI, 27 June 1963

THE transcripts of the unity talks make it plain that the euphoria that swept Arab opinion on 17 April was based on very little substance. In fact, anyone reading the agreement at the time with some sober reflection might grasp that rather little had really been decided, and that all that had been exchanged was a commitment to come to terms in the future. In an Arab world where for a generation constitutional formalities had had little to do with the realities of the political process, and where changes in regime often occurred in a sudden and unpredictable manner, the detailed elaboration of presidential, parliamentary, and regional powers contained in the agreement was less significant than the decision to delay their implementation for some twenty-five months. Much would happen during this period, politicians and parties might come and go—in Damascus and Baghdad, at any rate—and the form of the union, if it did come into being on schedule, would not necessarily have much to do with terms negotiated long in advance.

If discerning observers could draw such conclusions from the text of the agreement itself, even the simplest Arab citizen could understand when the transcript of the discussions was published that mistrust and disagreement had dominated the atmosphere from the first day, and that the agreement was not only unable to assure the future, but that it concealed a most unpromising present. But so compelling is the symbol of Arab unity, and so ready is the Arab mass mind to be lifted up yet once more to great expectations that are destined to be disappointed, and to assume that somehow this time it will be different, that the publication of the agreement was not received with the caution that its very text invited. It remained for political struggles in the coming months in Damascus and Baghdad, and for a propaganda battle culminating in Egypt's publication of the unity talks themselves in late June and July, to damp the public's elation and make it plain to them that 'unity of purpose' reflected in ideological slogans was no foundation in itself for the construction of Arab unity.

Aftermath in Syria and Iraq

The crucial struggle was in Syria where, unlike Iraq, the Ba'th and its rivals were already in a certain uneasy and fluid kind of balance. Although the Ba'th initially held the inside track, occupying the greater number of key positions in the NRCC and the cabinet, they were under considerable moral pressure to accommodate the other groups, especially after the Cairo talks. Under the pressure of crisis the proverbial divisions and intrigues of Syrian politics came gushing forth. The struggle was conducted not simply between the politicians of the various parties and within the army, but also within the Ba'th itself. As in previous years, each Syrian faction appealed for support from friends in Baghdad or Cairo who scarcely needed encouragement.

The precise terms of the coalition between the Ba'th and its rivals were not spelled out in the text of the Cairo agreement, and there was ample room for disagreement. Should equality of representation apply only to the directing committee of the projected political front, or also to the cabinet and the NRCC? Should 'equality' mean 50 per cent Ba'thists and 50 per cent from the other three organizations combined, or 25 per cent Ba'thists and 25 per cent from each of the others? Or should independents constitute a fifth element? Even if a formula should be agreed upon, it would remain to decide who should occupy which post. Then what would be the practical role of the Front committee? What would guarantee its influence over the decisions of the NRCC and the cabinet, which were the only bodies in which constitutional authority was vested? How should the committee arrive at decisions? Disagreements at various levels would surely erupt in time over successive policy decisions, especially amidst preparations for elections. It could not be foreseen to what extent each group might insist on its own views in each circumstance and threaten to disrupt the coalition.

Then there was the problem of the army. What would be the composition of its High Command, and who would have the last word on dismissals, promotions, and transfers? One might nominally agree that the army should be removed from politics; indeed, after Syria's dismal record of military coups, many civilian politicians might sincerely insist on it. But what would this mean? If it meant that GHQ should administer the army without interference from the politicians, then what assurance was there that politically or factionally minded officers would not carry on their intrigues on their own, elbowing their rivals out of positions of influence and then hiding behind the principle of the army's professional autonomy? In reality it was not the army that needed saving from the politicians, but the reverse. Syrian officers had become so habituated to the prospect of 'correcting' civilian regimes of which they disapproved that a given civilian political group, however respectable its intentions, was bound to keep an anxious eye on alignments and deployments in the army, and not to feel safe unless its own favoured faction of officers was in a secure or even dominant position. But then, the civilians might come to be dominated by their own military supporters. In course of time, this happened to the Ba'th.

The outcome of these uncertainties was bound to depend on the extent to which 'Abd al-Nasir might encourage his Syrian allies to drive a hard bargain with the Ba'th, or restrain them from doing so, and also on the Ba'th's own estimate of what they could afford to concede without jeopardizing their security. Since there is only fragmentary information about the negotiations in Damascus, it is hazardous to judge what the terms of this contest really were. Initially after the 8 March coup the cabinet had been formed under Bitar with Ba'thists occupying half the seats, while the majority of the NRCC were Ba'th members or sympathizers. Nihad al-Qasim, Hani al-Hindi, Sami Sufan, and their colleagues, who were accorded a lesser representation, accepted this arrangement for the time being, but already before the end of the Cairo talks they were pressing for rectification. Subsequently they published a memorandum declaring that 'before the delegation left for Cairo they agreed in a clear and straightforward manner with the Ba'th Party that activity in the proposed National Front should be on a basis of equality between the four groups'. The Ba'th, they complained, went back on this agreement.

Thus all that Mr Sami al-Jundi, the Minister of Information, has said about differences over the number of seats in the Cabinet and on the National Revolutionary Council is untrue. . . . These points were agreed on before the delegation

H

left for Cairo and the only mention of 'halves' and 'quarters' was in the mind of Jundi himself.[1]

But in fact it is clear that there were disputes over seats, although the precise formulation of the issue was and is a matter of some confusion. The bargaining had gone on since March, and various formulae were put forward at different times. This is reflected in the divergence of explanations of events conveyed to the author by a number of participants and close observers. The implicit common denominator of these versions is that an understanding was reached during or after the Cairo talks that the Ba'th and their collective rivals would each occupy an equal number of cabinet seats, with the balance to be held by independents, while in the NRCC the Ba'th would continue to hold half the membership. In Iraq, meanwhile, the Ba'th were expected to make some room for others, but it was taken for granted that this need only be nominal. The crucial issue in Damascus was thus the selection of independents, many of whom could be counted upon to lean in one direction or the other. The Nasirists objected to the Ba'th's list of favoured independents, and evidently with good reason. It was presumably with these independents in mind that Salah al-Din Bitar declared to the author with surprising (though incomplete) frankness that from 8 March onward the Ba'th Party unswervingly insisted on maintaining majority control for itself.

These disputes were tied to others concerning the 'political front' which was to direct the work of the NRCC and cabinet. The Cairo agreement specified that decisions in this body should be by majority (hence the Ba'th could presumably be easily outvoted); subsequently the Ba'thists variously demanded that decisions of the Front be unanimous or else of a merely consultative character (thus in either case leaving decisive power to the NRCC). One

[1] *APD*, p. 268.

Ba'thist present at the Cairo talks recalled that the provision in the agreement for majority vote had never been
settled in the negotiations but was slipped into the text at
the last minute by the Egyptians, along with the phrase
that implied that a unified single party would eventually
be formed. It does not seem possible in retrospect to establish the truth clearly regarding the disputes over the Front.

These questions were complicated by differences among
the non-Ba'thist parties. Just after the Cairo agreement
there were abortive negotiations between the Ba'th and
Sami Sufan's Socialist Unionist Movement, aimed at
bringing the SUM back into union with the Ba'th, from
which it had splintered off in 1961. Had this effort succeeded, an enlarged Ba'th could presumably have ad-
vanced a compelling claim to a preponderant position
vis-à-vis the remaining two movements. But just as the
negotiations were beginning to show some signs of success,
an event occurred which shattered this prospect and cast
a fateful shadow across all subsequent developments.

This was the abrupt move of the NRCC beginning at
the end of April to purge the army of a large number of
Nasirist officers. Some were retired from service, others
transferred to less sensitive posts. Among those dismissed
were the Minister of Defence, Lt-General Muhammad
Sufi, and the Deputy Chief of Staff, Major General Rashid
Qutayni. These measures followed a number of local dis-
turbances within the army between Ba'th and Nasir
partisans, in Aleppo and near Damascus; and in justifica-
tion of the purge the authorities alleged that a coup d'état
was being planned—a charge which the Nasirist leaders
hotly denied. Hindi, Qasim, Sufan, and others resigned
in protest from the cabinet, compelling Bitar's resignation
on 11 May.

Then there seems to have occurred a strange manoeuvre
described by a close observer as follows: Dr Sami al-

Jundi, a former associate of Sufan in the SUM but now friendly to the Ba'th, was entrusted by the NRCC with the formation of a cabinet. After two days he gave up the effort, complaining that the non-Ba'th groups had refused to negotiate despite his readiness to meet their wishes. They retorted that he had not consulted them. But meanwhile, behind Jundi's back, the NRCC had fastened their real hopes on Dr Sami Drubi, a moderate Ba'thist and Minister of Education in the outgoing cabinet. While in Cairo to attend an Arab League conference on education, Drubi consulted 'Abd al-Nasir; then he flew back to Damascus and worked out a settlement with the non-Ba'th leaders. Under his premiership they would receive a majority of seats both in the cabinet and the NRCC. The case of the dismissed and transferred officers would be reviewed impartially, that is to say presumably favourably, after a decent interval. This compromise plan was then laid before the Ba'th Party leadership, which rejected it. The affair was not disclosed to the public, who were left simply with the information that Jundi had tried and failed to form a government. Salah Bitar then returned on 13 May to form a cabinet dominated by the Ba'th and their friends.[2] (Six of the new ministers were Ba'thists and the other six reliably pro-Ba'th independents. Another six seats were left vacant for the other parties, who of course refused to occupy them.)

We cannot be sure of the accuracy of this strange tale. Other sources variously corroborated parts of it and denied others. Bitar would only confirm that Drubi had visited Nasir in Cairo; Atasi, that at one time Drubi's name among others was considered for the premiership; and Qasim, that it was proposed that Drubi should form a

---

[2] Related to the author by Nazih al-Hakim, former editor of the Damascus newspaper *al-Wahda al-'Arabiya*, sympathetic to 'Abd al-Nasir but a close friend of Drubi, as told to him by Drubi.

caretaker government of non-political figures to govern
Syria until the September plebiscite. What is certain is
that neither the Ba'thists nor their rivals took Jundi's
candidacy seriously, and that it served principally as a
cover for other more obscure manoeuvres. Perhaps the
Ba'th reckoned that it would be advantageous to display
Jundi's charade to the public so that it could be said,
truthfully if meaninglessly, that even a non-Ba'thist had
tried and failed to persuade the Nasirists to negotiate
reasonably.

Evidently the Ba'th leaders had concluded after the
Cairo talks that any serious concessions they made to their
rivals were likely to be used as springboards for further
demands against them, and perhaps for their removal
from the scene altogether. A really equal division of offices
with the others would deprive them of the last word in
Syria, and, to borrow 'Abd al-Nasir's phrase, place them
between the 'hammer and the anvil'. As for the army
purge, even if no coup had in fact been plotted against
them, it was always a possibility, especially as the crisis
among the politicians intensified. Their own strategy had
placed them in a dilemma: they had appealed for union as
a means of legitimizing themselves with the Syrian public,
and of guaranteeing themselves against Egypt's considerable means of harassment and subversion. For President
'Abd al-Nasir to look upon them with a benign eye would
be a major gain. On the other hand, the price he demanded,
for himself and on behalf of his Syrian partisans, was
dangerously high. Remembering their own experiences
with him under the 1958 union, such men as 'Aflaq and
Bitar could only be wary of another experiment, and it
seems clear that the party was divided between those who
were sincerely anxious for a new union as a matter of
ideological conviction, and those who at most would
accept union on highly favourable terms, which they failed

to obtain. But they could also consider Nasir's own experiences with Syria from 1958 to 1961, and surmise that
regardless of his oratory, he had no real wish for a new
entanglement either. Perhaps even his repeated insistence
in the Cairo talks on a broad sharing of power in Syria
could be discounted; perhaps in reality he would be satisfied to let the stipulated preliminaries of full constitutional
union drag out indefinitely, and leave control of Syria
substantially to the Ba'th, provided only that they kept a
nominal place in the government for those Syrian politicians who had put their trust in him. Had he not repeatedly
said during the Cairo talks that despite his misgivings, he
was agreeable to any form and degree of unity, from a
mere 'unity of objectives' upwards? Why, then, should the
Ba'th not present him with a *fait accompli* by seizing full
control in Syria as well as in Iraq, especially since it had
become clear that the Syrian Nasirite politicians, if not
Nasir himself, were determined to deprive the Ba'th of its
preponderance?

Thus on 6 May a Syrian army spokesman declared that
the purge of officers was no one's business but that of the
Syrian army itself. 'We will enter the union', he added
truculently, 'on the basis of our own circumstances in
Syria, not on a basis that is desired of us by others.' On
20 May a government source told the press that

> Syria considers the dispute existing between unionist groups
> to be a purely internal one which is capable of solution. It is
> therefore harmful to allow this dispute to reflect on and en-
> danger the cause of unity, and it would be better to leave it to
> be dealt with internally.

Other Ba'thists were dismayed that a party whose
mission it had been for twenty years to preach the gospel
of Arab unity should now find itself taking such a position.
Three men were notably absent from Bitar's second

cabinet: Drubi, Jamal al-Atasi, and 'Abd al-Karim Zuhur. Drubi and Atasi continued to serve the regime in lesser capacities;[3] Zuhur broke with the party altogether, went off in exile to Beirut, and publicly repented his previous positions. The 1958 union, he declared, should be reconstituted before anything further could be done. Viewed in the light of the Cairo talks, Zuhur's departure was a dramatic event. Of all the Syrian participants in the talks he alone had consistently shown courage, self-confidence, and intelligence in 'Abd al-Nasir's presence. Whether he was disillusioned by his colleagues' confusion or deviousness, or whether opportunism played a part in his decision, is a question we cannot answer. Known as an impulsive, wilful, and independent man, he is alleged in some quarters to have chafed under the somewhat exclusive leadership of 'Aflaq and Bitar, whose talent for political action he doubted (it is notable that he had entered parliament in 1954 as a protégé of Akram Hawrani in Hama). His conduct in Cairo, tenacious though it was, was evidently not in line with the cautious and conciliatory efforts that the party leaders had decided were tactically necessary. Possibly he hoped to gain credit within the party, after the collapse of relations with 'Abd al-Nasir, for having taken a hard line all along, and was then annoyed when his standing failed to improve; and indeed some prominent members of the party—but not 'Aflaq and Bitar— would have preferred to accommodate him. But he did not have his way and his defection was a moral victory for the Nasirists.

Throughout these events the Syrian government, as well

[3] After a time Drubi was appointed ambassador to Morocco, but immediately afterwards Syrian-Moroccan relations were broken and he spent four months in Rabat without presenting his credentials. In the autumn of 1964 he was offered an opportunity to become Prime Minister. He refused (the political situation in Syria was 'disgusting', he told a foreign journalist), and instead accepted the position of ambassador to Yugoslavia. Jundi served in several successive cabinets and eventually became ambassador in Paris.

as that of Iraq, continued to speak and act as if they still expected the fulfilment of the Cairo agreement. Indeed, they had to do so if they were to convey any impression that they had lived up to their commitments and that responsibility for the failure of union would lie with Cairo and its partisans. While pro-Nasir army officers were being rounded up, a number of measures were taken to bolster the regime's unionist and socialist image. A number of conservative politicians and officers were arrested and charged with the crime of the 1961 secession—a 'crime' which, we may recall, Salah al-Din Bitar himself had endorsed at the time—while others were stripped of their civil rights. The Syrian banks, nationalized in 1961 by 'Abd al-Nasir and denationalized after the secession, were now renationalized early in May. One reason given in the official explanatory declaration was that the banks were too large, and hence had tended to dominate successive governments; another was that they were too small, and hence hindered economic planning.[4] A third step was the adoption by both Syria and Iraq of a new flag with three stars, representing the union that was not destined to come into existence. (Egypt still flew a flag with two stars, representing the union that had broken up eighteen months before.)

In all these actions lay an element of absurdity, and this was fitting, for they were the product of an absurd situation in which symbols seemed to count for everything and reality for nothing. It was curious how the Ba'th spokesmen, while calling the Syrian Nasirists every manner of horrible name, could continue to declare their unswerving determination to unite with 'Abd al-Nasir himself, and to describe such a union as 'historically inevitable'. After suppressing an uprising of Nasirists in Aleppo, the Minister of Interior, Amin al-Hafiz, took to the radio to condemn

[4] Declaration of 5 May 1963 (*APD*, pp. 253–4).

'the dirty attempt and open plot against the people and against the future of the unity', carried out by 'a cheap group which practiced evil and stole the people's slogans' and whose purpose was 'to drown Aleppo in blood.'[5]

Thus only two weeks after the signature of the Cairo agreement the propaganda war was going full blast. The non-Ba'thist newspapers in Damascus were closed down, and two pro-Nasir editors were flung into al-Mazza prison alongside the secessionist politicians—that infamous dungeon in which prominent Syrians of all shades of the political spectrum had taken turns in inhabiting under various regimes, and of which General Luay al-Atasi, on the morrow of his own release from it, had cheerfully told 'Abd al-Nasir, 'We are going to turn it into a museum'. The newspaper *al-Ba'th* (14 June 1963) characterized Hasanayn Haykal, editor of Cairo's *al-Ahram* and well known to be a close friend of Nasir, as 'a provincialist, bureaucratic bourgeois whose mentality and interest contradict the thinking of true revolutionaries'. The Ba'th Party had decided, said the paper (26 June 1963), 'to bear the full responsibility for defending the unionist orientation and the construction of a sound union [with whom, one wonders?] in which there is no place for domination by stooges, opportunists, and *mabahithiyin* (agents of the Egyptian Secret Service)'.

In Iraq, where the Ba'th-led regime had also on 13 May reorganized itself, the invective heaped on pro-Nasir elements took a similar, if somewhat more colourful, form. Like its Syrian counterpart, the Iraqi NRCC claimed that its efforts at conciliation had been rebuffed:

The Revolution's many attempts to establish the National Front were met at times by deliberate and provocative attempts to set obstacles in the way of its establishment, at other times with delaying tactics intended to stultify this noble objective.

[5] Damascus Domestic Radio Service, 8 May 1963.

All of this came to pass in accordance with a planned conspiracy.

. . . The base attempts made by these groups were a prelude to the execution of their dastardly plot, the aim of which was to strike at the organizations that are now protecting the revolution, to destroy the National Guard, butcher the army, and attack all popular organizations. They wanted first to spread chaos and drown Iraq in a sea of blood, then strike down all progressive and unionist trends that emanated from the 14th of Ramadan Revolution and establish a reactionary dictatorial regime antagonistic to the people. People of Iraq: the elements that plotted against us are mere insignificant groups that are isolated from the people: 'movementists' [i.e. the Arab Nationalist Movement], reactionaries, stooges [of Nasir, presumably], opportunists, and other embittered elements that submitted to Qasim's regime.[6]

Such charges were not calculated to facilitate the task of building a coalition with the Nasirists. Nor was Baghdad Radio's imaginative commentary (25 May 1963):

Reactionaries, opportunists, and cowards have been harbouring hatred and baseness, and like frightened bats which fear light and which fear to face the people, went on disseminating venomous, black hatred and misleading rumours, reflecting their weak and opportunistic spirits. . . . The revolution will crush in its advance all the pygmies who stand in the way of the giants who guided the people toward their great future on the morning of the 14th of Ramadan.

Throughout May and June the Egyptian government maintained a correct silence, and the Cairo press and radio, while sharply criticizing the insistence of the Syrian Ba'th on monopolizing authority for themselves, and particularly the purge of non-Ba'thists from the Syrian army, did so with a relative dignity that suggested as much sorrow as anger. Syria was heading for a 'horrible disaster', *al-Ahram* warned on 14 May. Two days later it alleged

[6] *APD*, p. 275 (slightly modified).

that the Ba'th planned to provoke Egypt to withdraw from
the unity agreement, leaving the way open for a bilateral
union with Ba'thist Iraq. About Iraq the Egyptians said
very little. It was left to the 'Voice of the Arab Nation', a
clandestine radio broadcasting from Egyptian territory, to
answer the Ba'thists in kind on 26 May 1963:

> The blood of 'Aflaq and Bitar is the price of correcting the
> Ba'th Party's deviation. Kill these two traitors and you will
> have cut two long tails of British imperialism. Anyone who kills
> them will have done the Arab nation a service which Arab
> history will never forget.

Such were the voices of Arab unity, representing those
forces which had agreed to celebrate their 'unity of objectives' by forming coalitions.

The Syrian Ba'th took a further step to consolidate their
position by obtaining the dismissal and exile of Major-
General Ziyad Hariri, the Chief of Staff, on 8 July, after
two weeks of underhand manoeuvres that had begun
with the removal of thirty of his supporters among the
officer corps while he was away on a visit to Algeria. Perhaps only in the Syrian army could affairs be conducted
by resort to the strange intrigues used against Hariri: at
one point the Chief of Staff was forbidden to visit the
Syrian-Israeli front, where his partisans were concentrated.
Two Ba'th officers, Salim Hatum and Ibrahim al-'Ali, are
said to have urged him to organize a coup, and arranged
to smuggle him to the front for this purpose in the boot of
their car; but Hariri, correctly sensing that this was a trap
to expose him to charges of seditious insubordination,
prudently declined. None the less, after a few more days'
delay, the NRCC reconfirmed his dismissal. Oddly,
although Hariri's alleged ambitions had aroused the mistrust of Ba'thists and Nasirists alike, his chief friend in
court appears to have been Bitar, who saw him off at the

airport with tears in his eyes. Hafiz, already Deputy Prime Minister, Minister of the Interior, and Deputy Military Governor, now became Chief of Staff and Acting Minister of Defence as well, and was promoted to Major-General. He was rapidly emerging as the most powerful figure in Syria, and it remained only for him to replace Atasi as President of the NRCC and Commander-in-Chief of the armed forces on 27 July. The following November he was also to succeed Bitar and add the post of Prime Minister to his already incredible list of titles.

On 18 July, as General Atasi arrived in Alexandria to discuss with 'Abd al-Nasir the rapidly deteriorating Syro-Egyptian relations, a large-scale Nasirist *putsch* against the Ba'th regime occurred in Damascus. It was quite a different affair from previous coups. For one thing, whereas the classic pattern was for tanks to roll into Damascus at two or three o'clock in the morning and quietly arrest leading personages and occupy key buildings, on this occasion the attempt was staged at midday, when the population was in the streets, by means of a mixed military-civilian uprising within the city. Then, whereas on several previous occasions regimes confronted with revolts had peacefully, almost gracefully, collapsed, the Ba'th were determined at all costs to retain power. They made use of the tight grip on the army they had so assiduously developed and of their undisciplined National Guard to suppress the uprising by every means, including tanks, artillery, aircraft, and indiscriminately aimed tommy-guns. Estimates of the number killed—including a large proportion of innocent bystanders—ranged into many hundreds. In another innovation in the patterns of Syrian politics, the authorities promptly lined up twenty of those arrested against the wall and shot them. The pro-Nasir members of the first Bitar cabinet, General Qutayni, and other suspects managed to escape to Lebanon. A round-the-clock curfew was imposed in Damascus. Luay al-Atasi, who until now had represented a degree of restraint on the Ba'th's ambitions, saw in the events of 18 July the final collapse of his efforts and quietly relinquished his position to Amin al-Hafiz.

The Ba'th–Nasir breakdown

With the crushing of this attempt, the dialogue between 'Abd al-Nasir and the Ba'th that had begun with the Cairo talks was finished. Neither he nor they made any further pretence of intending to implement the 17 April agreement. Nasir, who until now had kept silence, devoted a speech on 22 July to a blistering attack on the Ba'th, declaring:

We do not consider that the UAR is bound to the present Fascist regime in Syria by any common aim. This...is impossible when the other regime is built on fraud and treachery, is non-unionist and non-socialist, but rather secessionist, inhuman and immoral. We do not consider that the Damascus Government represents the Syria with which we signed the Tripartite Union Agreement. Indeed this Agreement did not bind governments but revolutionary nationalist Arab forces.

Syria and the Syrian people are poles apart from the present Fascist regime. . . . We have therefore decided that this Agreement is valid only if the true Syria is a party to it but that the Agreement does not bind us in the least to the Fascist Ba'thist regime. . . . Our acceptance of this Fascist regime as a partner in Union would be tantamount to a betrayal of the cause of Arab Unity and of the Syrian people, who alone possess the right to settle the issue. . . . We cannot, nor can the Syrian people, presume to [unite] under the shadow of scaffolds, blood baths and collective massacres.[7]

'Fascism' was an epithet that had freely been applied a decade earlier to the Syrian National Social Party, in condemnation of its crude dogmatism, its exclusive and con-

[7] Ibid. pp. 332–3. For full text see *Nasser's Speeches, 1963*, pp. 118–56.

spiratorial organization, its aspirations to dictatorship, its penchant for violence, and its alleged affinities to British and American imperialism. The currency of the term testified in part to the rising prestige of the Soviet Union and its ability to provide the radicals of the world with slogans. If one takes the word to suggest the primacy of the will to power over disinterested concern for social and economic welfare, the Ba'th is not the only contemporary Arab nationalist movement to be touched by its implications. But 'Abd al-Nasir's appropriation of quasi-Marxist language to describe his socialist measures over the past two years, plus the Ba'th's inability during their brief and shaky period in power to enact significant social legislation, enabled him to fling the charge of 'Fascism' in their faces with seeming impunity.

The Syrian NRCC replied to 'Abd al-Nasir's attack with its own version of events, including an account of the Cairo talks which contradicted the text of the minutes that had been published in *al-Ahram* and broadcast on the Egyptian radio:

The major point of controversy was the political and democratic structure of the proposed state. Our delegation insisted on the necessity for a parliamentary regime based on representation proportionate to the population of each region. When the question of political representation came up, the Egyptian side insisted on equal representation for all unionist forces. When the Syrian side demanded the inclusion of all unorganized unionist elements in certain groups, this was rejected. The Egyptian side in turn emphasized the privileges and powers of the President.

We finally agreed to all these demands so as to avoid disruption of the talks, and in order not to disappoint the hopes of the Arabs.

It was, of course, to discredit Ba'thist versions of the talks in advance that the Egyptians had published the minutes, accurately or not. 'We published the records', Nasir had derisively remarked in his speech, 'so that Michel 'Aflaq should not go and sit in some coffee house and say, "I sat there talking for three hours and exposed their mental bankruptcy, and I expressed great ideas".[8] But the NRCC, striving to cast on to Nasir the odium for the failure of union, went beyond specifics in their statement and complained:

The Secessionists once claimed that they wanted no union with 'Abd al-Nasir. It grieves us, therefore, to hear him now proclaiming no union with the Ba'th. Unity soars above party and personalities. It is a historical destiny whose disruption constitutes a historical crime. The National Revolutionary Council insists on the implementation of the Charter and considers its abrogation, whether conscious or otherwise, to be tantamount to Secession.[9]

This exchange of condemnations was scarcely surprising. What was more curious, especially for the ideologically minded, was the lesson that 'Abd al-Nasir drew:

A natural, legitimate union is assured and inevitable, but this also requires that we analyse its rationale. We previously believed that progressive Arab revolutions render union probable. But nowadays the concept of Union is itself in crisis. I am beginning to feel that political revolutions do not automatically entail a union. Witness the case of 'Abd al-Karim Qasim, later to be followed by the Ba'th. Deviation, selfishness and spite have been the result of these revolutions. . . . In the past we stated that we would co-operate with all nationalist groups or organizations. But we have now been proved wrong. This kind of multiplicity of nationalist activities seems to lead us to clashes. . . . We must therefore begin to look ahead into the future and draw the proper lesson from these events. The future must be viewed in a new light. While every Arab country boasts a party, union seems utterly impossible. True political opposition would degenerate into regionalism, with

[8] *Nasser's Speeches, 1963*, p. 152.   [9] *APD*, pp. 356–7.

Syria at odds with Egypt, Iraq at odds with Syria, and so forth. For union to emerge, and for all immoral opportunist obstacles to be overcome, we must launch a unified Arab Nationalist movement which would incorporate all the nationalist movements of the Arab world.[10]

Thus the concept of the basis of Arab unity had been reduced a further step. 'Unity of ranks', a slogan embracing the co-operation of all Arab states regardless of their internal systems, had given way after September 1961 to 'unity of objectives', embracing all radical nationalist movements. Now it had been shown that socialists and revolutionaries were as capable of quarrelling with each other as they were with 'reactionaries'—perhaps more so, in fact, because radical militant organizations had a tendency to become prisoners of their own totalitarian ideologies and to see themselves as indispensable national saviours.

With the failure of the Damascus uprising of 18 July the Nasirists in Syria had expended their final reserves of organized strength. Those in the army had been weeded out or arrested; most of the civilian leaders had fled to exile in Beirut, whence they carried on a press and radio campaign against the Ba'th but without serious hope of stimulating further rebellions. Within Syria, the events since the 1961 secession had wrecked the moral credit of all groups: the traditional politicians for their selfishness and timidity, the Nasirists for their impotence and their inability to offer anything better than a return to the old Egyptian-dominated union of 1958–61, and now the Ba'th for their ruthlessness and conceit. The latter qualities, if not endearing to the public, none the less helped the party in power to tighten its grip.

Until 18 July the Ba'th-Nasirist quarrel had still retained certain fluidity, in that non-Ba'th elements were still

[10] Ibid. p. 333.

numerous in Syria, still organized and still able to some degree to compete for public favour and even to influence attitudes within the NRCC and perhaps the leadership of the party itself. The door to co-operation with Egypt had stayed open a crack: 'Abd al-Nasir had not publicly denounced the unity agreement, was still discreetly receiving emissaries from Damascus, and was still cautiously maintaining friendly relations with the Ba'th of Iraq, and thus an indirect link with the Syrians. In this situation it had remained important to the Syrian Ba'th to pay lip-service to the agreement and to Nasir personally, even while denouncing his 'stooges', and to defer public consideration of alternatives to the tripartite unity plan.

The 18th of July removed these circumstances. The Nasirites were gone. There was blood between them and the Ba'th, and 'Abd al-Nasir himself had declared war. Henceforth the Ba'th had no one's sensibilities to consider but their own. Even a tour of Egypt and Syria by President 'Abd al-Salam 'Arif of Iraq at the end of August, for the purpose of mediation, changed nothing: for 'Arif, though friendly to Nasir and not a Ba'thist, was still wholeheartedly contributing his prestige to the Ba'th-dominated regime over which he presided. The 'National' (i.e. inter-Arab) Command of the Ba'th Party now began publishing statements openly condemning the system of government in Egypt itself and promising to try to 'correct' it.[11] This was a newly avowed ambition, calling to mind the following interchange during the Cairo talks:

Nasir: What do you hope to achieve by this union: the correction of 'Abd al-Nasir's regime?
Bitar: No.
Nasir: Do you think this regime is good or bad?
Bitar: It is good, Your Excellency.
Nasir: Do you or don't you intend to correct it?

---

[11] See, for example, the statement of 17 Sept. 1963 (ibid. pp. 377–80).

I

Bitar: Not at all. What we want is an interaction of the two experiments of Syria and Egypt. . . .

Nasir: What Syrian experiment? . . .

Iraqi-Syrian negotiations

What was of much greater account was that shortly after 18 July the Ba'th leaders began to speak of the possibility of a bilateral Syrian-Iraqi union. Preliminary negotiations to this end were in progress before the end of August. Thus the Iraqi Ba'th also allowed their ties to 'Abd al-Nasir to lapse. On 11 October Nasir, in a letter to 'Arif, excused himself from a promised visit to Baghdad, on the grounds that the Ba'th manifesto of 17 September had been issued in the name of the National Party Command, which included leading members of the Iraqi government.

During 'Arif's visit to Syria an agreement for economic union was concluded, and on 8 October a treaty of military union was signed. The Iraqi Minister of Defence, Lt-General Salih Mahdi 'Ammash, became Commander-in-Chief of the united armies of the two countries, with headquarters in Damascus. Shortly afterward a Syrian brigade was sent to Iraq to participate in the operations against the Kurdish rebels in the north. The Sixth National Congress of the National Command of the Ba'th Party, meeting in Damascus, passed a resolution calling for full federal union between the two countries.[12]

A Syrian-Iraqi union could only be viewed with alarm in Cairo. This was not simply because of the context of events in recent months, of the struggle between the Ba'th and its Arab nationalist rivals in Damascus and Baghdad and 'Abd al-Nasir's repeated references during the Cairo talks to the prospect of a Ba'thist 'hammer and anvil'

[12] 27 Oct. 1963. Full text of the resolutions of the Congress, ibid. pp. 438–44.

between which Egypt might be caught in the event of a tripartite union, though all this was no doubt much in people's minds at the time. More fundamentally, such a union would spell defeat for a policy that successive Egyptian governments had unflaggingly pursued since 1944: the prevention of any Fertile Crescent unity from which Egypt might be excluded, and by which the primacy in inter-Arab affairs that Egypt had sought to maintain, first through the Arab League and later through the dynamism of her revolution, might be destroyed. Egyptian courtship of President Shukri al-Quwatli until 1949 and then of Husni Za'im, opposition to the Baghdad Pact and to Nuri al-Sa'id and Prince 'Abd al-Ilah, the cultivation of the Ba'th, the creation of the UAR, the hostility to 'Abd al-Karim Qasim and to the Arab Communists, and, finally, the maintenance of good relations with the Iraqi Ba'th as distinguished from the Syrian Ba'th—all these policies, and others, had aimed above all at forestalling the growth of Iraqi influence in Syria or the creation of a Baghdad–Damascus axis. Now, in November 1963, it seemed that Egypt was powerless to prevent it.

That a Syrian-Iraqi union failed to materialize was not due to any success of Egyptian policy but because of the ineptitude of the Ba'th. Unlike the Syrian branch of the party, the Iraqi Ba'th had been bred on conspiracy and violence in the days of Qasim, at whose hands they had suffered much, and they had wreaked bloody vengeance in their extermination of Communists after the 14th of Rama-dan. Almost in imitation of the much-hated Popular Resistance that had terrorized Baghdad on behalf of the Communists during the first two years of Qasim's rule, the Ba'th established their own para-military force, the National Guard, whose loyalty was carefully cultivated by the most ambitious of the civilian Ba'thists, the Deputy Prime Minister, 'Ali Salih al-Sa'di. In building up their

I*

strength and prerogatives, even to the point of possessing their own air force units, the National Guard increasingly antagonized officers of the regular armed forces, including high-ranking Ba'thists among them. The rivalry found its counterpart among the civilian party leaders as well. Some of them—notably Talib Shabib and Hazim Jawad—questioned the need for the Guard's existence and developed suspicions of Sa'di's intent to use it for his own political ends. They were also put off by his rough and contentious personality and by his tendency to disregard established party policies and procedures. In the cabinet reshuffle of 13 May they had managed to remove Sa'di from the Ministry of the Interior, whence he had helped the National Guard enlarge its prerogatives, and made him Minister of Information and National Guidance. But this post also he managed to use as an effective springboard for cultivating support for his ambitions.

On 11 November the Iraqi Regional Conference of the party met and abruptly dropped Sa'di and one of his supporters, the Regional Party Secretary, Hamdi 'Abd al-Majid, from the leadership council. They were bundled on to a plane bound for Madrid. Sa'di's supporters in the National Guard then broke into acts of violence, both against opposing elements in the Guard itself and, more recklessly, against the army. Two jet aircraft fired rockets on Rashid military base outside Baghdad and on the Republican Palace where Sa'di's opponents were gathered. A battle in the streets ensued until a compromise arrangement was negotiated by the Defence Minister, 'Ammash. Sa'di's ouster was confirmed, but in return Shabib and Jawad were induced to go into exile in Beirut. The Regional Party Command was dissolved, to be replaced for the time being by the direct authority of the National Command with headquarters in Damascus and represented equally by Syrians ('Aflaq, Hafiz, and Salah Jadid) and Iraqis (Bakr, 'Ammash, and Colonel 'Abd al-Sattar 'Abd al-Latif). The Syrians were summoned from Damascus to confirm this arrangement. Henceforth the Iraqi Ba'th regime, shorn of its principal civilian leaders, would be guided to a large extent from Syria. The NRCC, the supreme constitutional body in Iraq, had not even an opportunity to meet to undertake the formality of dismissing Shabib and Jawad, or for that matter Sa'di and 'Abd al-Majid, from the cabinet.

The 'Arif regime

Faced with this self-decapitation of the party and the army's anger at continued rebelliousness from the National Guard, President 'Abd al-Salam 'Arif moved into the breach on 18 November. He issued decrees in the name of the NRCC (which still did not meet) granting himself full emergency powers, dissolving the National Guard, and forming a new cabinet. Lt-General Tahir Yahya, the Army Chief of Staff, became Prime Minister and Air Force Commander Brigadier Hardan Takriti was made Minister of Defence. Major-General Ahmad Hasan al-Bakr, the outgoing Prime Minister, accepted the post of Deputy Premier.

These men were Ba'th members and had been prominent in the regime in the past nine months, but before long it became clear that Yahya, if not the other two, had abandoned the party and that with their acquiescence real authority had been placed in the hands of 'Arif, whose religious conservatism, lack of enthusiasm for socialism, and friendship with 'Abd al-Nasir had made him increasingly uncomfortable as an ornament of the Ba'th. The remnants of Ba'thist presence in the new regime soon disappeared, and much of the party's previous influence was inherited by its arch-enemy, the Arab Nationalist Movement. As early as 21 November 'Arif pointedly remarked at a press conference that no political parties had been granted permission to operate since the revolution of 8 February 1963 ('14 Ramadan'). Talib Shabib and Hazim Jawad, who made the mistake of returning to Baghdad from Beirut early in 1964 without authorization, were given lunch by the Prime Minister, Yahya, and then forced to board a special plane to Cairo to live quietly under the supervision of the Egyptian authorities. Salih 'Ammash had already been sent to Cairo in November. Eventually Takriti was relegated to Stockholm as Ambassador, and Bakr charged with complicity in a plot and jailed in Baghdad. 'Arif's new regime turned towards friendship with Cairo. Within a few weeks after 18 November the most vicious propaganda battle in the Middle East was no longer that between Cairo and Damascus, but between Damascus and Baghdad, as Syrians and Iraqis waved their identical three-starred flags in each other's faces.

5

Rebound: The Cairo Summit, January 1964

The concept of Arab unity no longer requires meetings of the rulers of the Arab Nation to portray solidarity among governments. The phase of the social revolution has surpassed that superficial concept of Arab unity.

THE UAR NATIONAL CHARTER OF 1962

AT the end of 1963 more Arab states were at each other's throats at once than ever before. Syria was feuding with Egypt, and, since November, with Iraq. Egypt and Saudi Arabia were locked in a struggle for the future of Yemen, where 40,000 Egyptian troops had failed to win a final victory for the revolution there. Algeria had come to blows with Morocco over a border dispute and had another dispute with Tunisia. Tunisia and Morocco had been cool to each other ever since Tunisia had recognized the independence of Mauritania. Egypt was hostile to Jordan, as well as Saudi Arabia, as a matter of ideological principle, and took the side of revolutionary Algeria against her more conservative neighbours. Syria deemed it ideologically fashionable to be unfriendly to Jordan and to Morocco, and was trading complaints with Lebanon over border incidents. Of the thirteen member states of the Arab League, only three were on satisfactory terms with everyone: Kuwait (towards whom Qasim's successors in Baghdad had relented), the Sudan, and Libya.

The majority of these quarrels, whatever their specific origins, pitted revolutionary against conservative or moderate regimes: Egypt, Algeria, Iraq, the Republic of Yemen, and Syria, variously, against the others. But of all disputes the most bitter and least soluble was between the rival revolutionary movements of Damascus and Cairo.

While these quarrels raged the Arab League was naturally powerless. The League had always been a useful vehicle for agreement when agreement was desired, and occasionally as a forum in which pressure could be brought against one lone black sheep, but its effective functioning had always required that a general desire for co-operation prevail. In the mid 1950s it had been paralysed by the struggle between Egypt and Iraq over the Baghdad Pact; then, after 1958, by the quarrel between 'Abd al-Nasir and Qasim. By 1962 first Iraq and then Egypt were boycotting the sessions of the League in pique over Kuwait and Syria respectively.

The more radical pan-Arabists had long complained that the Arab League was really an obstacle to Arab unity rather than an aid to it, because it sanctified the separate sovereignties of its members, and by forbidding them to interfere in each other's internal affairs it hampered the contagion of the revolution in Arab society which, to the minds of these critics, was the only solid basis on which eventual unity could be built. The rise of the Egyptian revolution after 1952 left an impression on Arab nationalist minds sufficiently deep and lasting to ensure that the League would never come to serve as the primary medium for inter-Arab relations or as the foundation for Arab solidarity, except when Egypt's own interests temporarily required it, or until such times as Egypt's rulers might modify their basic conceptions. For in the absence of such circumstances the mistrust between revolutionary and conservative regimes could be counted upon to keep the League chronically split. And as the Egyptian-Syrian-Iraqi struggle of 1963 suggested, the hatred of rival revolutionary Arab movements for each other could be even more crippling. 'Unity of ranks' had been discredited as a slogan; now even 'unity of purpose' had been proved inadequate.

But revolutionary movements as ambitious as that of Egypt have a tendency periodically to over-extend themselves. At times when hostilities reach their maximum an event may occur which suddenly brings the contestants to their senses. This had happened to the UAR at the end of 1958 and in 1959, in her relations both with the United States and (as we have seen) with Jordan and Saudi Arabia. It was after American-Egyptian tensions had mounted steadily since 1955—broken only briefly during the Suez war—and culminated in the landing of US marines in Lebanon, that the air had suddenly cleared, and from late 1958 to late 1964 there ensued a period of friendly co-operation. The catalyst—but not the only cause—had been 'Abd al-Karim Qasim.

Monarchs and Presidents

At the end of 1963, at the climax of Arab quarrels, an even more sudden and dramatic détente occurred. In mid-December the Cairo press was exchanging the usual insults with Damascus, Amman, and Riyad: three weeks later 'Abd al-Nasir was embracing Sa'ud and Husayn at Cairo Airport, and politely shaking hands with Hafiz. The kings and presidents of the Arab states had gathered in Cairo for a summit meeting of the Arab League and re-established friendship within the space of a few hours. The reconciliation fell short of settling all differences, but general cordiality and mutual tolerance returned, and with them the intended spirit of the League.

The catalyst on this occasion was Israel, which was approaching the completion of its project to divert the head-waters of the Jordan river from their natural storage basin, the Sea of Galilee. We shall not enter into the details of the long-standing dispute between Israel and the Arab states over the use of Jordan waters, but simply note here that no Israeli water diversion plans had ever won Arab acceptance, and that long before this particular plan was due for completion various Arab leaders had declared it to constitute an act of Israeli aggression against Arab rights and threatened to meet it by force. Such talk had been cheap in the years before the project was finished. In Syria especially, successive insecure regimes had found it a handy means of waving their Arabism in the faces of their critics, in the familiar Arab game of 'more anti-Israel than thou'. But now that the time of decision approached, commitments to go to war were seen to be very dangerous—especially in Egypt and Jordan, the two countries which could least afford to be dragged into a battle with Israel provoked by the Syrians. King Husayn would stand to lose his territory west of the Jordan, and probably with it his throne; 'Abd al-Nasir stood to lose prestige. He was in no position to fight, with half his army tied down in Yemen; but almost worse than military defeat would be the shame of doing nothing to help Syria or Jordan. Even if no one went to war at all, Nasir could still suffer grievously, for it was mainly to him that Arabs had looked, with his encouragement, to prevent Israel from carrying out another *fait accompli*. Nothing could so delight the Ba'th as to see Nasir deflated. Since Egypt was unready for war, it was essential to make other Arab governments publicly share moral responsibility for a decision not to fight—and concurrently to join in bringing pressure on the Syrians to hold their fire. Meanwhile there were suitable steps short of war that the Arabs could take, particularly the diversion of Jordan river tributaries in Syria, Lebanon, and Jordan so as to reduce the volume of water within Israel's reach; and here it was essential, for the sake of Egyptian prestige, for Egypt to share in the credit for this.

On 17 December the Cairo weekly magazine *Rose al-Yusuf* published an article containing two principal points. The first was that 'the United Arab Republic will not let itself be pushed into a battle with Israel before the attainment of unity among all the Arab countries'. The second point, which seemed to contradict the first, was that 'the UAR know how and when it will eliminate Israel, and it knows itself to be capable of shouldering this burden by itself'.

The Syrians, in company with 'Abd al-Nasir's other enemies, emitted cries of indignation. *Rose al-Yusuf*, 'the nationalized Egyptian magazine', had committed 'a great national crime which even the rotten reactionaries, the stepchildren of imperialism, never dared to commit'. Nasir was compared to Marshal Pétain who had surrendered France to the invader in 1940, and whom, it was pointedly noted, the French people had punished without regard for the glory he had previously earned at Verdun (i.e. like Nasir at Suez).[2]

While the Ba'th was still spluttering over *Rose al-Yusuf*, 'Abd al-Nasir was addressing the crowds at Port Said. After a routine castigation of Ba'thist 'immorality' and 'arrogance' he turned to the subject of Palestine.

In order to confront Israel, which put a challenge to us last week, and whose Chief of Staff stood up and said, 'We shall divert the water against the will of the Arabs, and let the Arabs do what they can', a meeting between the Arab Kings and Heads of State must take place as soon as possible, regardless of the strifes and conflicts between them. Those with whom we are in strife, we are prepared to meet; those with whom we have a quarrel, we are ready, for the sake of Palestine, to sit

[1] *al-Ba'th*, 19 Dec. 1963.   [2] Ibid. 23 Dec. 1963.

with. . . . We will sit and talk seriously at the meeting, and it will be no shame if we come out and say that we cannot today use force. We will tell you the truth, we will tell you every word that was said, that we cannot use force today because our circumstances do not allow us; be patient with us, the battle of Palestine can continue, and the battle of the Jordan is part of the battle of Palestine. Or we may say that we will be able, if they divert the waters of the River Jordan, to stop this diversion by force. But we will not say one thing behind closed doors and another thing outside. . . . For I would lead you to disaster if I were to proclaim that I would fight at a time when I was unable to do so. I would not lead my country to disaster and would not gamble with its destiny.

Let us try to forget all the stupidities and irritations which we have seen in the past few years; also the disputes that took place, the words that were spoken, and the treachery and so on.[3]

The next day the Syrian NRCC issued its reply. It complained that 'Abd al-Nasir's speech had been 'dominated by vituperation' and in return it reminded him of some of his latest sins, but added that co-operation in the face of the Israeli diversion plans was a national duty, and that therefore it would accept the invitation. It added its hope that propaganda campaigns could be terminated.[4] This wish was quickly fulfilled: within a few days the Cairo press and radio, scarcely pausing for breath, switched to describing the personal virtues and accomplishments of the men they had for so long been reviling.

In terms of the Egyptian requirements in the Jordan river question, the conference was a triumphant success. Of the dignitaries gathered in the Arab League headquarters, none expressed an interest in going to war except Amin al-Hafiz, who was effectively put in his place by a succession of other speakers. Plans for diversion of

[3] *Nasser's Speeches, 1963*, pp. 311–12 (trans. slightly adapted).
[4] Text of statement in *al-Ba'th*, 25 Dec. 1963.

the Syrian, Lebanese, and Jordanian tributaries of the Jordan were set in motion, and a joint military defence command established under Egyptian leadership. It did not matter that the Arab diversion operation would take years to complete and might not, in any case, deny Israel the share of water she required: the most important need of the moment had not been the diversion of water but the diversion of the Syrian government from any hope of immersing Gamal 'Abd al-Nasir in war or embarrassment.

Other reasons for the Cairo Summit

We have spoken of the Jordan waters question as a catalyst in the process of Arab reconciliation. No doubt it was the main immediate reason for summoning the Cairo Summit Conference, but there were other broader reasons, related to results that were of considerably greater significance than the decisions taken regarding Israel.

The Egyptian revolutionary government, confronting a host of reactionary foes and, in the case of Syria, a revolutionary competitor, seemed to have found by December 1963 that its most strenuous efforts were enough to cause its antagonists a great deal of discomfort but not enough to sweep them from power; or even if it might manage here or there to do so, not at least in a manner which would assure it any control over the consequences. It was small comfort that the harassment of Sa'ud, Husayn, and the Ba'th was more difficult for these people to sustain than their counter-propaganda was for the Egyptians; what mattered was the ultimate futility of continuing to rail against regimes without tangible results. There appears to have emerged in Cairo, as it had sporadically in the past, the glimmering of consciousness that positive influence over other governments' policies may be obtained more easily by conciliation and tolerance than by threats or abusiveness. Then, too, there was the continuing Yemen stalemate and its ruinous expense to the hard-pressed Egyptian economy. One of the major results of the Cairo Summit was the resumption of Saudi-Egyptian cordiality and the initiation of a serious effort to negotiate a compromise settlement in Yemen. A year later success had still not been achieved, so narrow a field for concessions had Egypt's previous deep commitment of her prestige allowed her; this was a testimonial of the over-extended ambitiousness of the policies that in January 1964 Egypt sought, belatedly, to correct.

With Syria the road to mutual forgiveness was more difficult, despite the fact that there were no particular material problems to be solved, and despite the fact that the press and radio battle between the two countries, which was the principal manifestation of hostility, was mercifully cancelled by both sides. Hafiz was received at the Cairo Summit correctly but coldly. The only other head of state with whom he managed to meet privately was 'Abd al-Salam 'Arif—which was curious, inasmuch as of all Arab states it was Syria and Iraq that were the least reconciled to each other after the Cairo conference, and between which propaganda warfare continued. 'Abd al-Nasir avoided meeting Hafiz privately, and diplomatic relations between Cairo and Damascus, which had never been re-established since Syria's departure from the UAR in September 1961, were not resumed. The cold war between Cairo and Damascus had been ended only in the negative spirit of a truce, with expressions of cordiality restricted to the exchange of congratulatory telegrams on national holidays. (A mild improvement occurred at Alexandria in September 1964, at the close of a second summit conference, when Nasir invited Hafiz to lunch. At the time of writing this remained the high point in relations.)

Why was it easier for President 'Abd al-Nasir to resume friendship with the conservative monarchs of Jordan and Saudi Arabia than with his revolutionary socialist counterparts in Damascus? One might imagine that one reason was that the monarchs, conscious of being unpopular anachronisms in a radical age, had a greater craving to be loved in Cairo, and were therefore more ready to respond warmly and co-operatively to Nasir's overtures than were the self-sufficient Ba'thists with their dogmatic certainties. Yet the Ba'th had every practical reason to wish for warmer relations with Egypt than they obtained; and both Hafiz's conduct in Cairo—he stayed on an extra day in the vain hope of seeing 'Abd al-Nasir—and editorials in *al-Ba'th* seemed to bear this supposition out. For one thing, Egypt and Iraq were now beginning to draw increasingly close together, in the wake of the expulsion of the Ba'th from Baghdad, and it had become the turn of the Syrians to think about a 'hammer and anvil'. For another, the Ba'th had achieved their minimum aim of consolidating their control of Syria; they now hoped for Cairo's acquiescence. The silent reception they received at the Cairo Summit signified an Egyptian acknowledgement of their position, but not quite an acceptance of it.

The reason for the continued coolness lay in Cairo rather than in Damascus, and just as the Ba'th's conception of their interest can be traced back to the Cairo unity talks, so also can 'Abd al-Nasir's. He could mend relations with Husayn and Sa'ud because he had no acknowledged moral claims on them. He and they knew that he could resume hostilities at any moment of his choosing; in the meanwhile they would be glad of his friendship, and would do what they could afford to accommodate him. With the Ba'th his relationship was different. They were fellow radicals with whom he had already bargained for terms of collaboration, in negotiations that were now a matter of public record; the terms they had sought, and were still seeking now, would have constituted a threat to his own leadership and prestige in the Arab world, and he had rejected them. At least formally, they had seemed to accept his terms, and then managed not to honour them, for their prestige and pretensions to leadership at least locally had been at stake also. How, nine months later, could he give his blessing to the division of spoils he had previously spurned, whereby the Ba'th would run Syria while he ran Egypt? He could not prevent their running Syria, but he had no cause to congratulate them.

The military dictatorship

In the contest for the control of Syria 'Abd al-Nasir had been defeated, though not disgraced. He had not staked his reputation on winning, but only on preventing the Ba'th from using him, and on preserving the moral independence from the Ba'th that he needed for leadership in the wider Arab arena. The Cairo Summit Conference had been a striking demonstration of such leadership.

For the Syrian opponents of the Ba'th it was less easy to accept the outcome of the struggle. 'Abd al-Nasir had his own country to run; all they had salvaged was their dignity, which was small consolation for the fact—underlined by the Cairo Summit—that without strong moral and material support from Egypt they had ceased to count for much on the Arab scene. In 1964 the pro-Nasir Syrians in Beirut and Cairo regrouped themselves in a new organization called the Arab Socialist Union, named in imitation of the Egyptian mass organization, with Nihad al-Qasim as Secretary-General. Despite occasional flurries of activity—Qasim's repeated trips to Cairo to visit President 'Abd al-Nasir, and a prolonged closed-

doors convention in Cairo in May 1965—it was difficult
to see what prospects the organization possessed except
as a club for exiles, as long as the Egyptians did not really
help them to overthrow the Syrian government. There
was something forlorn about the predicament of its better-
known members, men in their thirties and forties such as
Hani al-Hindi, Luay al-Atasi, and 'Abd al-Hamid Sarraj,
who had held high office for a time and were now condemned to an indefinite period of obscurity and inactivity.

What did Qasim consult 'Abd al-Nasir about, and what
was discussed at the organization's meetings? No one
would say, but one could surmise that the Syrian exiles
were pleading for more positive Egyptian backing, and
chafing among themselves in frustration. The ageing
Nihad al-Qasim yielded the leadership of the ASU to
Jasim Alwan, the young ex-colonel who had directed the
disastrous 18 July uprising in Damascus. Meanwhile some
erstwhile colleagues stood aloof: Sami Sufan returned to
live unobtrusively in Damascus, and 'Abd al-Karim
Zuhur, the fierce individualist who had quit the Ba'th in
May 1963, in turn quit the ASU, complaining that it was
a waste of time.

Amidst these unpromising conditions there was ample
time for the Syrian Nasirists to ponder the lessons of their
failure. Retrospectively, the chief question was whether
they had been wrong to accept a subordinate position in
the Ba'th-led government after 8 March 1963, and to
accept the Ba'th's formula of tripartite negotiations for
unity instead of insisting on first reconstituting the union
with Egypt. By associating themselves with the Ba'th on
the Ba'th's terms, had they not invited the Ba'th to ex-
ploit them and thereby consolidate its grip on Syria? There
were various answers to this question. Hani al-Hindi
averred emphatically that this had been his view from the
start, that he had joined the government against his better

judgement and that events had proved him right. Nihad al-Qasim, however, believed that at the time there had been no honourable alternative to pursuing every hope, however slim, of co-operating with the Ba'th in quest of Arab unity. 'They are both right', General Atasi remarked to the author. Yet despite Atasi's evident desire to dispel any suspicion of Ba'thist sympathies that might arise from his record in office ('I warned Hafiz and the others repeatedly that they were leading Syria down a blind alley, in defiance of duty and of the logic of history'), he expressed the view that just possibly a chance had been missed. Had the Nasirists been patient enough to accept Ba'thist predominance until the plebiscite scheduled for September, the union would have come into formal existence. Once this happened, it might have proved difficult for the Ba'th to cling to their position—unless they were prepared to secede, and to bear the onus for so doing. But this logic could easily be stood on its head.

As for the Ba'th Party, while successful in fending off 'Abd al-Nasir and the Nasirists in Damascus, it suffered a serious moral impoverishment. The party had traditionally stood in the forefront of the appeal for Arab unity; now it was isolated in Syria, scarcely on speaking terms with other Arab unionist elements and incapable in the foreseeable future of contributing anything positive to the unionist cause. In the name of Arabism it had succeeded only in shutting off Syria from friendship with her neighbours.

Secondly, the party had championed democracy, civil liberties, and civilian rule. It had earned credit in this respect in resisting Adib Shishakli's dictatorship, and its criticism of 'Abd al-Nasir's rule in Syria after 1958, while not exactly disinterested, had had a certain ring of honour and sincerity. But by 1964 it was difficult to see important distinctions between the rule of Major-General Hafiz and